IRELAND

Lush green meadows and gentle
hills, dreaming lakes and moors,
stunning rocky coasts, remote
cottages, bustling cities, musicians,
pubs and Guinness – Ireland.
Ballynahinch Lake in Connemara.

IRELAND

Victorian charm: Take a one-horse "jaunting car" for a comfortable, leisurely trip exploring the beauties of Killarney National Park in County Kerry in the south-west of the "Green Isle".

ABOUT THIS BOOK

"Ireland, sir, for good or evil, is like no other place under heaven; and no man can touch its sod or breathe its air without becoming better or worse." Thus Keegan, a character in the comedy *John Bull's Other Island* (1904) by the Irish playwright and Nobel laureate George Bernard Shaw (1856–1950), on his native Ireland, expressing the author's views.

Ireland, the more westerly of the two large British Isles, has many names. "Ireland" is its official name in English and "Éire" in Irish. Its lush green meadows and trees have led to its being called "the Green Isle". More frequently heard today is the metaphorical epithet "the Emerald Isle". The island owes its year-round green vegetation to a mild, moist climate tempered by the Atlantic Drift. The beautiful scenery is what stuns visitors at first. A hard edge and a soft center – you might describe Ireland's geological features this way because the mountains are in the far east and west, with a rocky coast framing a center that consists of green pastures, boggy moorland and glittering lakes. From Donegal in the north to Kerry in the south, a spectacular coastline boasts Europe's highest sea cliffs, countless coves and sandy beaches, rocky headlands and remote off-shore islands lashed by Atlantic storms. More than 1,500 years ago, monks sought out this rugged country on the fringes of the then known world and converted its people to Christianity. Ireland is rich in artefacts and architecture attesting to its glorious Celtic past, including beautifully worked stone crosses, the exquisite Book of Kells and massively built monastic establishments, built for the ages. No less fascinating are the myths and traditional music. Sit back in a cozy Irish pub nursing a glass of Irish whiskey or a pint of stout, black as peat, and hear the stories and songs of Ireland.

This guide presents the riches of the fabled Emerald Isle. The atlas section that follows makes it easy to find the places and sights you want to see and adds a wealth of pointers useful for visitors. The index at the end, linking the picture section and the atlas pages, also includes the Internet addresses of the most important sights so you can get your bearings more quickly. Discover the magic of Ireland in all its diversity.

The Publisher

Anyone planning to circumnavigate Ireland faces a long trip (3,172 km/ 1,971 miles). As in all island societies, fishing has a long tradition. The port of Portmagee, a village in County Kerry.

CONTENTS

Ireland is divided into four historic provinces: Ulster condenses the attractions and the contradictions of the entire island. Connacht, once impoverished, is today known for its enchanting mountain scenery and coastlines. Leinster is home to historically interesting sites. And Munster provides many high points of a trip to Ireland in a single region. The provinces are subdivided into 32 counties. The Republic of Ireland has 26 counties; Northern Ireland six.

Devenish Island is uninhabited but boasts the impressive ruins of churches and monastic sites dating from the 12th–15th centuries, a round tower (25 m/82 ft) and a small museum. On a spectacular but precarious perch, Dunlace Castle, built high above the sea, has been uninhabited since 1639, when the kitchen fell into the sea and a kitchen boy was the sole survivor.

ULSTER

The province of Ulster unites the attractions and the conflicts of the island. Of the nine Ulster counties, three belong to the Republic of Ireland and six are part of the United Kingdom and Northern Ireland. Part of the Republic of Ireland, Donegal in the west is known for its rugged coastal scenery. The Northern Ireland counties are lovely, even, on the Antrim coast and in the Mountains of Mourne, spectacular. Since the armed conflict between Catholics and Protestants ended, Belfast, the capital of Ulster, has flourished.

Broad, barren moors are typical of the Donegal north coast. Ling and Bell Heather, also a popular garden plant, are amongst the few plants to thrive here. The white, silky tufts of Cottongrass or Cottonsedge also dot the moors. From the 16th century the Clan Sweeney sought refuge in Doe Castle because it was surrounded on three sides by the sea. The four-storeyed tower house was inhabited until as late as 1909 and members of leading families are buried in the Doe Castle cemetery.

The north coast of Donegal

The northern coast of Donegal is still a sparsely settled, lonely stretch of country. But to earlier clan chiefs it evidently did not seem remote enough to provide adequate protection from enemies, which is why a massive stronghold was built in the 16th century: Doe Castle on Sheephaven Bay, built by the Clan Sweeney. The notorious Tory Island pirates, who for centuries were a threat to shipping in these waters, were better protected against incursions. After terrible storms in 1974, Tory Island seemed to be in irreversible decline. The efforts of a Jesuit priest, however, have ensured that now more than a hundred people live on the island, which is about 5 km (3.1 miles) long. The Horn Peninsula, with high cliffs (200 m/656 ft), on which puffins and storm petrels nest, is one of the most beautiful of the many headlands in northern Donegal.

Thanks to the unstable weather conditions along the Atlantic coast, magnificent rainbows are not a rare sight – here at Fanad Head Lighthouse on the Donegal peninsula of that name. Visitors don't have to be romantics to rave about this view: evening at Fanad Head with the Fanad Head Lighthouse. Quite a few people are convinced that County Donegal has the most beautiful scenery in Ireland.

Fanad Head Lighthouse

Fanad Head boasts a varied scenery and a coast with alluring sandy beaches, as at Portsalong on the east side, some wooded areas and remarkable rock formations, including the Arch of Doaghbeg, a natural arch north of Rathmullan. The site of Fanad Head lighthouse, which has a powerful beam visible far out to sea, is also spectacular. Despite its romantic appearance, the lighthouse, like almost all others today, is electronically controlled and has no lighthouse keeper. The nearby Carmelite Friary in Rathmullan was the setting for a scene in 1607 that would represent a turning-point in Irish history. The flight of the Earls, Tyrone (O'Neill) and his ally O'Donnell, from the English forces opened the way to the Jacobean "plantations": the north of Ireland was settled with Scottish Protestants, laying the groundwork for the "Troubles".

Glenveagh National Park featuring Glenveagh Castle is a high point of any visit to Donegal. Exotic imported trees and Mediterranean flora thrive in the Castle gardens, as does a large herd of red deer.

Mount Errigal, the region's tallest peak (750 m/2,461 ft), rises from the middle of the National Park. When visibility is good, you can see all the way to the western province of Connacht from the summit.

Mount Errigal and Glenveagh National Park

Lough Beagh, a long lake, is the focus of Glenveagh National Park. The scenery and the view of Mount Errigal are idyllic but the National Park has a disgraceful history. Captain John Adair, a land speculator with an American wife, bought the land in the 19th century and had over 200 tenant farmers evicted not long after the disastrous potato famine, leaving them to go to the poorhouse or emigrate to Australia. In the 1870s Adair built a handsome Scottish Baronial-style castle on the lake shore. His widow had gardens laid out and kept a herd of red deer on the estate. In the 20th century, Henry P. McIlhenny, a Philadelphian of Irish descent, bought the estate and enlarged the park. In 1981 he compensated to some extent for his predecessor's conduct by giving the castle and grounds to the Irish state. They are now open to the public.

The views from Horn Head to the Rosquill Peninsula are unforgettable. The region is sparsely settled and lonely, as suggested by the hulk of a ship in "The Rosses". Fanad Head is a craggy peninsula with beautiful scenery. Further to the west is Bloody Foreland Head, dotted with the occasional solitary farmstead and cottages.

The west coast of Donegal

The west coast of Donegal, with its cliffs and sandy beaches, may be beautiful, but the hinterland is barren. Sheep graze gorse and heather, providing wool for sturdy tweed cloth. The nearby town of Ardara is an important base of the Irish tweed industry. "The Rosses" (meaning "The Headlands"), is a region north of Ardara, described by the satirical novelist Flann O'Brien (nom de plume of Brian O'Nolan) as barren and famished country. However, retired people from other parts of western Donegal, whose pensions have enabled them to build houses with sea views, have brought modest prosperity. The small island of Arranmore has a population of well under 1,000; the cries of gulls are virtually the only sounds to disturb its peaceful quiet. Guiding mariners since 1798, the Arranmore lighthouse in the northwest is the oldest on this part of the coast.

Lonely country at Glencolumbkille with the ruins of an early church and pre-Christian standing stones. Towards Donegal are the Slieve League cliffs, Europe's highest, and the fishing village of Killybegs. The stark sea-washed coastal formations along secluded Glen Head, near Glencolumbkille have a dramatic appearance. From here the end of the world really doesn't seem far ...

The south coast of Donegal

The white houses of the fishing port of Killybegs cover the slope above the town. The spectacular steep grey Slieve League cliffs to the west are the highest in Europe. In the 6th century, St Columba (from Old Irish Columcille: "Dove of the Church"), a native son of Donegal who brought Christianity to Scotland, chose this lonely coast to found a monastery. Every year on June 9, the saint's feast day, a procession of penitents takes place in his memory. From lonely high moors with sparse vegetation, you descend to the fertile valley of the River Murin. Despite its superlative beach, Glencolumbkille seems like the end of the world. Because it is so isolated, this coastal region is a Gaeltacht, one of the regions recognized by the Irish government as predominantly Irish-speaking, where Irish is the language still spoken in the home.

The attractions of the Inishowen Peninsula at a glance: a sweeping scenic vista with steep coastal cliffs, here at Malin Head. Broad valleys and plains form the green landscape around the Lough Swilly fjord.

The Grianán of Aileach is a trivallate cashel hill fort, whose name translates as "Stone Palace of the Sunny View". Ptolemy of Alexandria may have known of this puzzling fort in the 2nd century AD.

Inishowen

The Inishowen Peninsula lies between two fjords at the northern tip of Ireland: narrow Lough Swilly in the west and broad Lough Foyle in the east. Slieve Snaght ("Snow Mountain") is the highest peak in the local mountain chain. Inishowen has deserted beaches and numerous prehistoric ruins. The most stunning archaeological site is the Grianán of Aileach, a unique trivallate cashel hill fort; its name ("Stone Palace of the Sunny View") has led to conjecture that it was once a temple of the sun. The earthworks were built about 3,700 years ago but the stone walls date from historic times. The Kings of Ulster from the O'Neill clan lived here. In 1101 Murtagh O'Brien took the fort and had it razed. The walls were not restored until the 19th century. This breathtaking vantage point affords beautiful views over the rolling countryside and Lough Swilly.

Portrush on the Causeway Coast is a lively, quirky seaside resort town, situated on a promontory jutting out into the sea. The silky sand- dunes near Portrush offer an irresistible invitation to take long, contemplative walks away from the bustling town.

Portrush

The town of Portrush in County Antrim looks like a typical UK seaside resort. Attractive guesthouses from the Victorian era provide bed and breakfast and the long sandy beaches are perfect for family holidays. The central part of town is on a peninsula and popular leisure activities, including an amusement park, abound in summer. But Portrush doesn't hibernate in winter. Many students from the University of Ulster have their lodgings there, in preference to nearby Coleraine, which is not a particularly appealing university town. Although fishing no longer plays much of a role in the local economy, the port is still the focus of the town. East of Portrush are the White Rocks, dramatically eroded cliffs of white limestone with a long cave, known as "Cathedral Cave". Surfers also appreciate this section of the Northern Ireland coast.

The turbulent history of Dunluce Castle and the Clan MacDonnell perfectly matches the romantic setting of the Castle perched high above the sea.

Dunluce Castle

In the 16th century, Dunluce Castle, built on the edge of a basalt cliff, was the stronghold of Sorley Boy MacDonnell, a descendant of the Scottish MacDonalds, who had made conquests in Ireland. MacDonnell defended his castle with cannon salvaged from the wreck of the *Girona*, a galleass from the Spanish Armada. Valuables and artefacts retrieved from the wreck are now displayed in the Ulster Museum in Belfast. One of Sorley Boy's sons finally professed allegiance to the English crown and was created Earl of Antrim. The next generation of MacDonnells left Dunluce of their own accord. After the kitchen collapsed into the sea in 1639, a catastrophe survived only by a kitchen boy, the Earl's wife found the sound of the waves unbearable and insisted on leaving. The MacDonnells moved to a more commodious castle at Glenarm.

At the Old Bushmills Distillery, everything is done in the traditional way: The only ingredients of this distinctive whisky are – apart from yeast – Irish barley and water from St Columb's Rill. The whisky is distilled in huge copper pots. The Old Bushmills Distillery does the distilling, blending, maturing and bottling of their proprietary whiskys all under one roof. Naturally you can enjoy a tasting at the distillery.

BUSHMILLS DISTILLERY

A town on the north coast of County Antrim, not far from the famous Giant's Causeway is sacred to whisky-lovers all over the world: Bushmills. The spirits distilled here bear the same name. The world's oldest whisky distillery was licensed in 1608. *Uisce beatha*, "water of life", anglicised to "whisky" and written as "whiskey" in Ireland, goes back even further, to the Middle Ages at least. The Irish regard their Scottish cousins as neophytes in this field. Irish emigrants to America spread the fame of Bushmills and the distillery had their own sailing vessel to transport their prize export across the Atlantic. The Bushmills Distillery was one of the few in Ireland to survive the effects of Prohibition (1920) in the US. At the Old Bushmills distillery, all stages of production are carried out in Victorian buildings on the premises. Distilled three times, this is a silky smooth whisky. Since the malt is not dried over an open peat fire, the peaty, smoky taste so characteristic of Scotch whisky is entirely lacking. The top of the range Old Bushmills product is aged for 21 years before finally being bottled in three different types of used cask: American bourbon barrels, then oak casks that have contained sherry and, finally, Madeira drums. Its bouquet and flavour are so subtle that they beggar description.

Since 1986, the Giant's Causeway has been designated a UNESCO World Natural Heritage site and, since 1987 a National Nature Reserve. This column formation is of volcanic origin and is the most important of its kind in the world.

Some of the most remarkable of the rock formations found in the spectacular Giant's Causeway bear metaphorical names, including the "Giant's Boot", the "Camel's Hump", "the Chimney Stacks", and the "Wishing Chair".

The Giant's Causeway

The celebrated Giant's Causeway was created more than 60 million years ago by a volcanic eruption under the sea. The molten lava congealed into about 37,000 columns, most of them hexagonal. The name "Giant's Causeway" recalls a legend explaining the origin of this bizarre rock formation. The giant Finn McCool built the Causeway to reach Scotland without getting his feet wet. There are similar rock formations with lava columns on the Scottish island of Staffa. Some versions have the giant falling in love in Scotland; according to others, he wanted to kill a Scottish giant. When Finn McCool saw that the Scottish giant was stronger, he returned via the Causeway and had his wife disguise him as a baby. The approaching Scottish giant was so terrified when he saw the enormous baby that he retreated and destroyed the link to Scotland.

Rugged, often steep, limestone cliffs are characteristic of the beautiful Antrim Coast, although in many places, as here at Whitepark Bay, there are also stretches of sandy beach with dunes.

Benbrane Head, a prime destination for walkers, is on the north Antrim Coast. You need to have a good head for heights to take the high footpath along the cliff edge.

The Antrim Coast

Scenic mountains dominate the landscape in much of County Antrim. Where they meet the sea, they form a rugged coast. The most important town on the north coast is Ballycastle, a pretty little port with a beach. Ballycastle is known for having the oldest Irish annual fair, which has been held since 1606: horses and sheep are sold at the Lammas Fair in August. Ferries run between Ballycastle and Rathlin Island, which is less than 25 km (15.5 miles) from the west coast of Scotland. The island had a violent history from early times. The first Viking assault on Ireland took place here in 795, when the island church was pillaged and its buildings burnt. In the 16th century English troops massacred the women and children of Clan MacDonnell. The next blood-bath suffered by the MacDonnells was the work of the Scottish Clan Campbell in 1642.

Several public buildings in Belfast, including City Hall, built in 1906, bear witness to the city's heyday over a century ago. The Stormont parliament building was built in the 1930s.

Belfast has a young population with a high percentage of students, which ensures a vibrant and varied nightlife. The music scene here is particularly creative and lively.

Belfast

Belfast, the capital of Northern Ireland, made dismal headlines for over thirty years. The armed struggle of the Irish Republican Army (IRA) for a united Ireland and the unrest arising from Protestants of Scottish descent loyal to the British crown marching through Catholic residential areas in the city shaped the media image of Belfast. Since the late 1990s, however, the conflict has not been played out with bombs and bullets and Belfast has begun to breathe freely. A spate of building activity attests to a boom, especially in Laganside on the banks of the river. The Parliament of Northern Ireland (Stormont) is to the east of the city. The statue in front of it commemorates Edward Henry Carson, Baron Carson, a Dublin Protestant, who was against home rule for Ireland in the early 20th century and was instrumental in keeping Ulster in the United Kingdom.

The Victorian interior of the Crown Liquor Saloon is a riot of hues with mosaics and stained-glass windows: tiles with polychrome patterns, walls hung with brocade, lavish wood-carving and a red granite-topped bar.

The celebrated Belfast Crown Liquor Saloon is both a museum and a pub: a side entrance leads to Flannigan's, a quieter bar on the first (US: second) floor featuring some exhibits salvaged from the legendary *Titanic*.

THE CROWN LIQUOR SALOON

Few pubs have been a listed by that venerable British institution, the National Trust, which is mainly committed to preserving stately houses and landscaped gardens. But with its grand historic exterior and its Victorian interior, The Crown Liquor Saloon in Belfast certainly deserves this tribute. Although quite conservative, the National Trust allowed itself to be persuaded by John Betjeman, among others, that a magnificent "Gin Palace" was just as worthy of preservation as a ducal seat. The Crown Liquor Saloon goes back to 1826, when it was called the Railway Tavern. The son of the second owner had voyaged far and wide and was interested in architecture, and gave the building a facelift in the 1880s and 1890s. For pub-crawlers who prefer discretion, the snugs are just the thing, with the added attraction of gas lighting and engraved stained-glass windows. The high quality of the workmanship both outside and inside is attributed to a number of Italian artisans, who at that time worked on decorating the interiors of Irish churches. During "The Troubles" – the armed conflict in the latter half of the 20th century – the Crown Liquor Saloon survived the bombing of the Europa Hotel located directly opposite and, after its restoration in 2004, benefited from the flourishing Belfast nightlife.

Where green banks and the Irish sky are reflected in water, dreams of tranquillity come true: Lower Lough Erne. On Devenish Island, at its southern end, a Romanesque round tower, oratory walls, a 13th-century church and a priory (15th and 16th centuries) recall a monastic past.

White Island, reached from the Castle Archdale marina, is another interesting monastic site, with a ruined 12th-century church and eight mysterious Early Christian stone figures and a mask. They definitely pre-date the church but their age and significance are the subject of conjecture.

Devenish Island and Lower Lough Erne

In County Fermanagh the River Erne winds through wooded hills to form two lakes, a paradise for lovers of nature, angling and sailing. Upper Lough Erne is a labyrinth of shallow bays and small islands hidden in reeds. Lower Lough Erne, on the other hand, widens out to provide a panoramic vista. Monks settled on this natural waterway, which pilgrims passed on their way to a shrine consecrated to St Patrick in Donegal. St Molaise founded the original monastery on Devenish Island at the southern end of Lower Loch Erne in the 6th century. In its heyday there were 1,500 novices here. For a thousand years the island, which was raided by Vikings in the 9th century, was renowned for its Christian scholarship. Among the ruins, which cover a wide area, there is an intricately carved high cross, one of the most beautiful in Ireland.

The grounds surrounding the manor house of Mount Stewart fall into different sections, ranging from unlandscaped scenery to a wide range of meticulously laid-out themed gardens. A walk to the Temple of the Winds opens up a beautiful view of Strangford Lough. The Mount Stewart garden was partly modelled after the landscape architecture and contemporary garden design of other European countries: the themed sections include a Spanish garden and an Italian garden featuring Mediterranean and exotic subtropical plants and flowers.

Mount Stewart Gardens

Mount Stewart House and Garden recall the era of the Anglo-Irish "ascendancy". It belonged to the Stewart family, whose heirs were Marquesses of Londonderry. Several of them figured prominantly in UK politics. Viscount Castlereagh, second Marquess of Londonderry, represented the UK as Foreign Secretary at the Congress of Vienna. He had the effrontery to send home the magnificent chairs that had been used by the delegates. Even more interesting than the house, furnishings and paintings are the gardens, which the wife of the seventh Marquess of Londonderry had laid out in the 1920s. She extended her themed scheme in the house to the grounds. There are Sunken, Spanish, Italian and Shamrock Gardens and the famous Dodo Terrace. The Gulf Stream ensures a mild, moist climate, ideal for growing tall trees and exotic vegetation.

The Mourne Mountains are almost uninhabited and roads are few and far between. The range is of volcanic origin, formed of multihued granite which scintillates wonderfully in the dappled light.

The origins of Dundrum Castle are obscure: some say the original fort on the site was built for the Knights Templar. After John de Courcy built his massive castle in 1177, it remained impregnable for centuries.

Dundrum Castle and the Mountains of Mourne

From a distance the Mountains of Mourne have rounded contours. However, climbers find plenty of challenges here and hill-walkers enjoy the solitude of the sparsely settled region, an area of outstanding natural beauty. The peaks, including the highest, Slieve Donard (850 m/2,789 ft), are bare with wooded lower slopes. The best view of the mountains is from the east coast, or from the shores of Carlingford Lough to the south. North of the mountains the village of Dundrum is dwarfed by the massive ruins of Dundrum Castle. Only a century after the Norman Conquest of England in 1066, John de Courcy, an Anglo-Norman adventurer, set his sights on Ireland. He built a castle here in 1177 but the stone walls still visible today may have been the work of his successors. Oliver Cromwell's troops took the Castle in the 17th century.

Ross Errilly Friary, a ruined 14th-century Franciscan abbey, stands on the shores of wide Lough Corrib. Most of the Abbey buildings still standing, however, date from the 16th century. When forcing the Irish to leave their homes and land, Cromwell is alleged to have decreed "To Hell or to Connacht, go where you like", in denigration of this barren region between Shannon and the sea.

CONNACHT

Connacht was one of Ireland's poorest regions when the English drove the Irish before them into this region in the 17th century. Now the province boasts some of the island's most remarkable scenery. The Irish cultural identity is rooted in the beautiful Aran Islands off the Atlantic coast, the lovely coastline and mountains of Connemara, the bustling city of Galway, and the nearby County Sligo, linked with the great lyric poet William Butler Yeats, who won the Nobel Prize for Literature in 1923.

The mists veiling Benbulbin conceal the Fianna warriors of the Fenian cycle of Irish legend, who are said to be sleeping on it. The Mullaghmore Peninsula, with its fine beach and small port, is a paradise on earth.

The ruins of the monastery on Inishmurray Island once held the notorious Clocha Breaca: Large round Cursing Stones, now inactivated, one hopes, and housed in the National Museum in Dublin.

County Sligo

The green hills and lakes of County Sligo provide a welcome contrast to the barren landscapes of the counties of Mayo and Donegal nearby. Benbulbin, an Ice Age rock formation, is the highest point in Sligo, visible from quite far away although it is not very high (527 m/1,729 ft). Inviting sandy beaches at Mullaghmore and good surfing conditions at Easky make the Sligo coast a popular holiday destination. It was much lonelier 1,400 years ago when St Molaise founded a monastic establishment on Inishmurray. Uninhabited since 1949, the island boasts the impressive ruins of a large monastic settlement, a pilgrimage destination until recently. At this well-preserved site, enclosed by a high (3–5 m/9.8–16.4 ft) wall three metres (9.8 ft) thick, you can vividly imagine the doughty monks defending themselves against marauding Vikings.

Sligo, the capital of County Sligo, is the most important city in north-western Ireland. A stylish town, Sligo is also a comfortable place to be, at least in the evening when the streets are quiet after the day's bustle. Sligo has been a major regional crossroads since the Middle Ages. Carrowmore, a cemetery of almost 60 megalithic tombs, surpasses all other prehistoric Irish megalith cemeteries in size and age. The most striking is an unexcavated structure, capping a rock formation close by: legend has it that this is Queen Maeve's final resting place.

Sligo town

Sligo (population: 20,000) is the largest town in the north-west of the Republic of Ireland. William Butler Yeats, Nobel laureate for 1923, is its most famous son. The greatest lyric poet in English in the late 19th and early 20th century, Yeats was born in Sligo in 1865, always returning to it from Dublin and travels abroad. A patriot steeped in Celtic mysticism tempered by a passionate love of nature, Yeats wrote his best known poem about an island in Lough Gill, a short walk from Sligo town. In "The Lake Isle of Innisfree", the poet yearns for the simple life on Innisfree. Sligo's sole medieval building, Sligo Abbey, is a ruined Dominican friary, but witnesses to a far more distant past . Some of the tombs in the megalithic cemetery of Carrowmore near the rock formation of Knocknarea are more than 5,000 years old.

The Rata Santa Maria Encoronata, a merchant carrack in the "invincible" Spanish Armada of 1588, was stranded at Blacksod Bay on the Mullet Isthmus; its crew seized two castles but most never saw Spain again. The old cemetery at Blacksod Point is a chilling memento mori.

Under open skies and accessed by narrow roads, the Mullet Peninsula, which is shaped like a lobster claw, is a forbidding landscape dotted with numerous remains from days long past: prehistoric megalithic tombs, earthworks and magical stone circles that never fail to captivate visitors.

The Mullet

High annual precipitation may explain why County Mayo is one of the less visited counties of the Irish Republic. Mayo was always poor and the condition of the topsoil near the Mullet Peninsula suggests why this was so. The road travels beyond Belmullet through peat bogs, until it reaches a flat isthmus with little vegetation. The Atlantic coast is rugged, but the east side, towards Blacksod Bay, is more protected. The few people here live in lonely farmsteads. There is no town life. The Mullet is peppered with prehistoric megalith monuments and early medieval Irish ringforts, such as Doonamo. Ringforts are generally believed to be Dark Age but derive morphologically from earthworks and causewayed forts. The most impressive site in the area is a few kilometres to the east: at Belderrig archaeologists are excavating a Neolithic village from a thick layer of peat.

One of the most beautiful stretches of coast is the beach at Keel, which is 3 km (1.8 miles) long and abuts the Cathedral Rocks. Here, the cliffs were formed by wind and wave into columns and caverns that look like church architecture. Achill Island has long been an inspiration for artists. The peat bogs and heather form a tapestry of muted shades, and the remains of the deserted village at Slievemore on the north coast, possibly abandoned during the Great Famine, are poignant.

Achill Island

The largest Irish island is linked to the mainland by a bridge. Well into the 20th century, the inhabitants of Achill Island spoke only Irish and the eastern half of the island is an official "Gaeltacht" region in which the language still predominates. In the 16th century, the famous "Sea Queen of Connacht", Grace O'Malley (ca 1530–1603), a real-life pirate queen and a worthy contemporary of Elizabeth I of England, had a base at Kildavnet Tower on the east coast. Artists have always been drawn to the solitude of the island. The Irish painter Paul Henry came for a visit in 1910 and stayed for nine years. The English writer Graham Greene is said to have finished the novel *The Heart of the Matter* in a cottage at Dooagh. German Nobel laureate Heinrich Böll, who had a house on the island, describes his impressions of life on Achill in his "Irish Journal".

Once a very rich region with a flourishing linen industry, the coastline of Clew Bay, scattered with drumlins (drowned whale-shaped hills), is now a solitary but beautiful area near the pretty town of Westport. One guest at Westport House was a celebrated university drop-out: Thomas De Quincey, author of "Confessions of an English Opium-Eater"; satirical novelist William Makepeace Thackeray also spent time here.

Clew Bay

The town of Westport is an oasis of urbanity in a bleak hinterland. Stately Georgian houses, a square with a market hall and a town hall all indicate that this was an 18th-century "planned town". By the early 19th century, Westport had seen better days because the competition from textile factories in the industrialized north of England was too strong for Irish looms. One of Ireland's most elegant houses is set in a park on the shores of

Clew Bay: Westport House, built in 1732, family seat of the Earl of Altamont, Marquess of Sligo. The family is proud to own a Rubens "Holy Family" and revels in a family tree that goes back 13 generations to Grace O'Malley, the Sea Queen of Connacht, definitely one of the most entrepreneurial and emancipated women in history, who amused Elizabeth I, herself no slouch in the bossiness department.

Rhododendrons and ancient trees line the path winding down to the little church on the shore. A walk up the hill to the Sacred Heart monument is worth the effort for the reward of the superlative views out across the valley. Kylemore Abbey stands on the shores of a beautiful lake near Kylemore and nestles into the hill behind. It was erected in the 19th century as the country seat of a prosperous entrepreneur.

Kylemore Abbey

After you have crossed the high moor, where peat-cutters still practice their traditional trade, the well-tended grounds of Kylemore Abbey make a welcome change. In the mid-19th century an affluent entrepreneur and politician had this dream castle built in the Neo-Gothic style for his young wife. Since no one could afford to maintain a residence on this scale with 33 bedrooms, Kylemore Abbey has housed a Benedictine convent and a girls' boarding school since long before the second world war. The public does have access to some rooms, including the library and the dining-room. A recent improvement has been the restoration of the Victorian Walled Garden with its greenhouses. Flowers and herbs thrive there – just as they did when Mitchell Henry, who had the house built, had them laid out to delight his bride.

The Connemara National Park was established in 1980 to preserve this unique region of blanket bog, heathland and mountains in its natural state. Well-marked footpaths make the park accessible to visitors. Information is available in Letterfrack.

The northern slopes of the Twelve Bens, or Twelve Pins, are in the Connemara National Park. Benbaun (718 m/2,355 ft) is the highest peak in the park and in County Galway. Ruins show that the lower flanks were once settled.

Connemara National Park

Connemara in western County Galway boasts scenery of a breathtaking, almost mythical beauty. Blanket bog spreads between two mountain ranges, the Twelve Bens and the Maamturks, and on three sides it is framed by a lacy coastline fringed with islands. To preserve this region, so typical of western Ireland, a stretch of land covering 20 sq km (7.7 sq miles) on the north-western slopes of the Twelve Bens was designated the Connemara National Park. As refreshing as this thinly populated region may be for stressed urbanites today, it was an inhospitable place for those trying to eke out an existence there in the past. Many gave up the unequal battle for subsistence on the barren land during the Famine of the 1840s, when the potato blight and other factors put paid to agriculture. Most of the emigrants went to North America.

Even today, Connemara is one of the most unspoilt, albeit barren, and wild regions in Ireland. Bounded by the Atlantic on three sides, the county is home to a modest local fishing industry. Thinly populated and remote, Connemara is dotted with lakes. Ferries runs from Connemara to Inishbofin, a tiny island off the indented coast at Horn Head. Beautiful sandy beaches and fine cliffs as well as some interesting historic monuments, including "Oliver Cromwell's Fort", make the island an attractive day-trip destination for visitors.

The west coast of Connemara

Fresh Atlantic breezes and a beautiful situation above the mouth of the River Owenglin against the backdrop of the Twelve Bens make Clifden the most popular place on the west coast of Connemara. The largest town in western Galway, Clifden is renowned for the live music in its pubs. In August each year visitors come from far and wide to the popular Connemara Pony Show. These small, sturdy ponies are a cross between native equines and Arabian horses from Andalucia. As no outsiders coveted the barren soil of Connemara, the Celtic culture persisted for a long time here. Oliver Cromwell was the first invader, in the 17th century, but he was not there for economic reasons: he drove his adversaries back to western Connemara and the nearby island of Inishbofin. "Oliver Cromwell's Fort" still stands on that small island, whose population has since dwindled to 200.

Like tweed, Connemara comes in many subtle shades, ranging from the scarlet and brown heathland at Killary Harbour, to the rich greens of bracken and ferns on Derryclare Lough, and the greys of the rugged cliffs near Maam Cross. Clifden, the largest town in Connemara, is a lively market town and, with a fine beach nearby and lovely scenery, it is a popular tourist destination. Visitors enjoy making the trip to abandoned Clifden Castle about 1.3 km (1 mile) out of town.

The Clifden hinterland

Forbidding mountains, lakes and a blanket of bog predominate as soon as you leave the Connemara coast. This is harsh country, scattered with granite outcrops. The scenery is green again along Lough Corrib, the second largest lake in Ireland and the largest in the Republic of Ireland. Anglers fish for salmon and trout here and the uninhabited island of Inchagoill, with its two ruined churches, attracts visitors. Long after the Celtic clan structure had decayed, the Martin family from Galway bought property in the Clifden hinterland. Almost two centuries ago, Richard "Humanity Dick" Martin, an early animal rights activist, built the castle on an island in Lough Ballynahinch as his family seat. Along with many of the poor, the Martins lost everything in the famine years and Richard Martin's second son emigrated to Canada with his large family.

The south coast of Connemara is fissured and indented, unravelling into a wet stony desert gashed with lakes that change seamlessly into a sea dotted with islets: the picture shows the rocky coast at Glinsk and at Lettergesh Beach.

Remote Lettermullen, in the far south, across from the fabled Aran Islands, is one of the host of small Connemara islands that are really headlands and promontories. Solitude is guaranteed here, especially in the off-season.

The south coast of Connemara

Patrick Henry (Pádraig) Pearse, teacher, barrister, poet and fiery Irish patriot, chose the lonely south coast of Connemara as his summer home. A leader of the 1916 Easter Rising for Irish independence, Pearse was executed. Now many patriotic Irish visit his old home in the tiny village of Rosmuck as a place of pilgrimage. Rosmuck is also known for its deserted sandy beaches. Dog's Bay and Gurteen Beach to the west near Round-stone are celebrated for their crystalline waters and soft sand. Roundstone fishermen catch lobster, crab and mackerel for a living and earn a little money on the side accompanying saltwater anglers who want to test their skills against tuna and sharks out on the Atlantic ocean. Errisberg mountain rises behind the town, its summit affording breathtaking views of the Connemara coast and moors.

Known as the "gateway to the west", bustling Galway straddles the banks of the River Corrib, linking the lake of that name with the Atlantic. For those in search of much more than peace and quiet, Galway is certainly the right place to be in western Ireland.

Ferries run from Galway Bay (not Galway city) to the Aran Islands – tides and weather permitting. While waiting to embark, fortify yourself for what may well be a rough crossing in one of the enormous choice of pubs…

Galway city

Galway is at the heart of the Irish cultural scene. Students and hordes of visitors ensure a pulsing nightlife, and not just in summer. The pubs and the city's music scene are legendary. The Oyster Festival in September, when piles of oysters are washed down with Guinness, is popular with locals and visitors alike. Anglo-Normans wrested the fort of Galway from the King of Connacht in the 13th century as a bulwark against the Irish tribes in the west of the islands. In medieval times, thank to its port and situation on the River Corrib, Galway became important for its trade with France and Spain. The Anglo-Norman Lynch family was so powerful that no one wanted to execute James Lynch's son for the murder of a Spaniard in 1493. He hanged his wayward offspring himself – a possible etymology for the term "lynch law".

Typical of the Aran Islands are the magnificent stone forts dating back to prehistoric times. The largest fort is on the island of Inishmore but huge Dún Fearbhaí, on Inishmaan (unusually, a rectangular fort), also known as Dún Moher, is hard to beat.

Isolation has ensured that the Aran Islands are strongholds of Irish Gaelic culture. Traditions that have died out elsewhere have survived here. The islanders earn their livelihoods from tourism, fishing and the famous Aran Island knitwear.

The Aran Islands

The three inhabited Aran Islands epitomize the demands of life on the Irish Atlantic coast. The public discovered the islands in the 1890s when playwright John Millington Synge set *Riders to the Sea* (1904) on one of them and described the way of life in articles and a journal. Consisting of limestone and a thin layer of topsoil and grass, the Aran Islands represent the geological continuity of the Burren karst limestone plateau. The remains of pre-Christian stone forts and early Christian churches show that the islands were always fortified against invasion. The largest island, Inishmore, is an inclined limestone plateau. Walls in elaborate dry-stone patterns like those on the famed Aran Island jumpers protect fields from storms. Inishmaan, rocky and undeveloped, and the smallest island, Inisheer, are also rich in relics of the past.

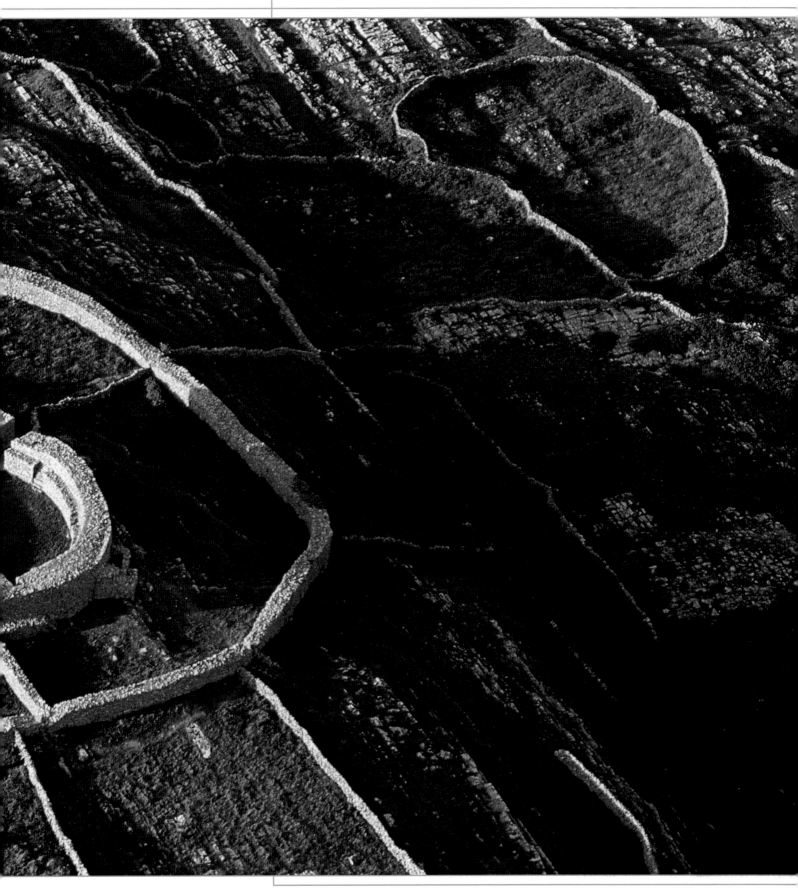

Anglo-Norman Roscommon Castle, built in 1269 for Roger d'Ufford, Lord Justice of Ireland, changed hands several times before being handed over to Cromwell's troops in the mid-17th century; all that remains of it are the corner towers and a double-towered gatehouse.

Boyle Abbey, which dates back to 1142, was the first successful Cistercian foundation in Ireland. The church, remodelled in the 15th century, contains the tomb of Felim O'Conor, King of Connacht in the 13th century: the king and eight of his retinue are depicted on it.

County Roscommon

As County Roscommon has no coastline, it is often overlooked by visitors. Its historical importance is, however, enormous: grave-mounds, forts and other monuments that may have been used for ritual purposes dating from the Bronze Age to the Middle Ages surround the old seat of the Kings of Connacht at Tulsk. A great many surveyed archaeological sites that have yet to be excavated might shed some light on the legends that abound in the region. According to Irish mythology, the Warrior Queen, Medb (Maeve), had her palace here. Bearing witness to recent history, the original Stable Yards at Strokestown Park House (ca 1740), once the seat of the Mahon family, now house a Famine Museum documenting the horrors of the 1840s, when starvation and emigration reduced the population of Ireland from eight to five million.

Clonmacnoise has something of the cemetery about it with its ruined buildings and high crosses. Several churches dating from the 11th to the 13th centuries are dotted about the site. The Old Library of

Trinity College is a highlight of the Republic of Ireland's capital. It contains 4.25 million book volumes, thousands of manuscripts, including sheet music, and the fabled "Book of Kells".

LEINSTER

The province of Leinster is known for its variegated scenery and important historic towns and cities, including Dublin, capital of the Republic of Ireland. Rolling hills, farms and moorland make up the green heart of the Emerald Isle. The beauty of the coastal mountains of County Wicklow is unspoilt. Leinster is rich in treasure from Irish history: the holy place of the High Kings at the Hill of Tara, the splendid Boyne Valley passage graves, and the medieval city of Kilkenny.

Three high crosses stand in the ruins of Monasterboice: Muiredach's High Cross (10th century), named after an abbot, with scenes of Adam and Eve, David and Goliath, Moses and the Life of Christ; the Last Judgement is depicted in the middle. The West Cross is also richly decorated. After

King Henry VIII of England disbanded monastic establishments from 1536, Mellifont Abbey became the fortified seat of the Counts of Drogheda. Damaged during a siege in the 17th century, the old abbey is in ruins: a lavabo, where monks washed their hands, and a chapter house remain.

Old Mellifont Abbey and Monasterboice

The fertile valley of the River Boyne near the town of Drogheda was a prime location for monastic establishments. Monasterboice, founded ca 500 by St Buite, is famous for its high crosses and one of Ireland's tallest round towers. Round towers are said to have been built as refuges for monks when Vikings attacked: the round form made them impregnable once the ladder to the high entrance was drawn up inside. High crosses were status symbols for monasteries and local aristocrats alike, serving as "Stone Bibles": Scripture could be explained to an illiterate populace from the scenes chiselled into them. Mellifont Abbey, founded in 1142, was the first Cistercian monastery in Ireland. Even in its ruined state, Mellifont recalls a glorious past as the main Cistercian abbey in Ireland, and founder of several of the 30-plus Irish Cistercian establishments.

Originally encircled by 127 kerb-stones, the largest Neolithic burial mound (60 m/196.9 ft in diameter) at Knowth is surrounded by 17 satellite tombs. Picture below: decorated stones; right: a passage in the Newgrange passage grave.

Newgrange, the largest, oldest (3,000–2,900 BC) and best-known burial mound in Ireland, consists of a massive kidney-shaped dome of stone and earth. It is encircled by twelve large kerb-stones, of which there were probably originally 38.

The Bend of the Boyne

On a bend of the River Boyne is one of Europe's most important prehistoric sites, a conglomeration of 40 Neolithic megalithic monuments. The burial mounds of Newgrange (predates the Great Pyramid at Giza and the Stonehenge trilithons), Knowth and Dowth, some of which date back more than 5,000 years, are the best-known. The Newgrange passage tomb (height: 13m/ 42.7 ft; diameter: 80 m/262.5 ft) may have been a burial site, a temple of the sun or an astronomical calendar. Neolithic spiral, wavy and other motifs decorate the massive kerb-stones (length: 4.5 m/14.8 ft) encircling the mound. Above the entrance is a small space that is touched by the rays of the rising sun at the Winter Solstice. The passage grave at Knowth may have been aligned so that it was illumined at sunrise on the spring and summer equinoxes.

The Irish folk music tradition is alive and thriving in many places – at regularly scheduled music festivals all over Ireland and in everyday life, in the street and live in numerous pubs throughout the island. The main instrument is the versatile fiddle. Other typical instruments used to round out the Irish sound are the tin whistle, the bodhrán (a flat hand-held frame drum), the guitar, banjo, accordion and concertina.

IRISH FOLK MUSIC

Irish pubs are known worldwide – for their inimitable casual ambience, often excellent live music and hearty stouts and beers. What happens at a pub evening with live music? A notice is hung out announcing music for the following evening at 8 pm. Arriving there on time, you wonder why nothing is happening. A handful of people with instruments turn up, the music starts, the Guinness flows and the mood takes off. Finally, guests show off their musical talent along with the band. The Irish love for music is self-evident and the traditions are manifold. Classical Irish music includes unaccompanied singing and instrumental music for dancing. What you hear at pubs tends to be some variant of folk music played on a variety of instruments. The boundaries between it and other kinds of music are blurred. American-inspired "Country and Irish" music is often heard. That the Irish love and talent for music also extends to Rock and Pop is convincingly demonstrated by the versatile and prolific Van Morrison and Sinead O'Connor and bands such as U2. Traditional Irish folk music is most often encountered in the Irish-speaking areas of the west at events put on by Comhaltas Ceoltóiri Éireann, an organisation dedicated to promoting Irish music, singing, dancing and the Irish language.

Trim Castle was the strongest Norman fort in Ireland. During his second expedition to Ireland in 1210, King John of England visited Trim. King Richard II of England kept his successor, Henry of Lancaster, prisoner here.

The Irish kings convened in the 3rd century to elect a High King on the Hill of Tara. The Stone of Destiny, which was said to roar its approval of their choice at the new king's touch, still stands here.

Trim Castle and the Hill of Tara

Ireland possesses more than its share of myths going back to prehistoric times. Many of the myths mention the sacred Hill of Tara, which looks back on 4,000 years of history, and which, in its heyday, was the seat of the High Kings. St Patrick celebrated the Christianising of Ireland in 433 by lighting a holy Paschal fire on the nearby Hill of Slane. King Laoghaire had forbidden him to do so as long as a festival fire was burning on the Hill of Tara. Almost a million people gathered at a "monster meeting" near Tara in 1843 in support of Daniel O'Connell's campaign for the repeal of the Act of Union (1801) with Great Britain. All there is to be seen on Tara today are grass rings and slopes, but a few kilometres away the skyline is dominated by an important landmark, symbolic of Anglo-Norman rule in Ireland: Trim Castle, dating from the late 12th century.

The Irish capital at night: the elegant Ha'penny (Halfpenny) Bridge, a foot bridge dating from from 1816, the Customs House and O'Connell Bridge (1794–1798), which is nearly as broad as it is long. Mount Street also looks splendid at night with its handsome Georgian houses. St Stephen's Church (1821) on Mount Street Crescent is also known as the "Pepper Canister" or the "Pepper Pot" church.

Dublin

Since the 1990s, Dublin has undergone an unprecedented upturn because the Irish economy has grown faster and for longer than any other in the European Union. New attractions for the younger generations have sprung up to rival venerable standbys such as the famed 18th-century Dublin Georgian architecture. In the part of Dublin known as Temple Bar, chic galleries, bars and restaurants are brimming with the new millennium lifestyle. The boom does have its negative sides such as congested streets and the sterile gentrification of picturesque old sections of the city. A settlement had existed on the River Liffey for centuries before the Vikings fortified it in the 9th century. From 1170, Dublin was the stronghold of the Anglo-Normans representing the crown of England. In 1921, it became the capital of the independent Republic of Ireland.

Anglican St Patrick's Cathedral, reconstructed in the late 19th century, is a Dublin landmark and Ireland's largest (93 m/305 ft long) church. Another equally celebrated Dublin building is the Old Library at Trinity College. Founded in the 16th century by England's Queen Elizabeth I, Trinity College is still the most prestigious Irish university. Scholarly visitors are drawn to the wonderful Old Library, which houses a wealth of fabulous illuminated manuscripts and old books.

Trinity College and St Patrick's Cathedral

Some historic Dublin buildings recall the Protestant English dominance over Celtic, Catholic Ireland: when Elizabeth I founded Trinity College in 1592, it was for the Protestant Ascendancy. Catholics were not permitted to study there until 1793; not until 1873 were Catholics admitted without being subjected to tests of loyalty to the Crown. The high point of this Neo-Classical university is the Long Room of the Old Library. Some 200,000 old books and the world-famous late 8th century "Book of Kells", the four gospels illustrated and explained in an illuminated manuscript, are kept here. Another Dublin highlight is St Patrick's Cathedral. Dating from 1220 to 1270, it was reconstructed in the late 19th century. It has been Anglican since the 18th century. Jonathan Swift, author of "Gulliver's Travels", was dean here from 1713 until 1745.

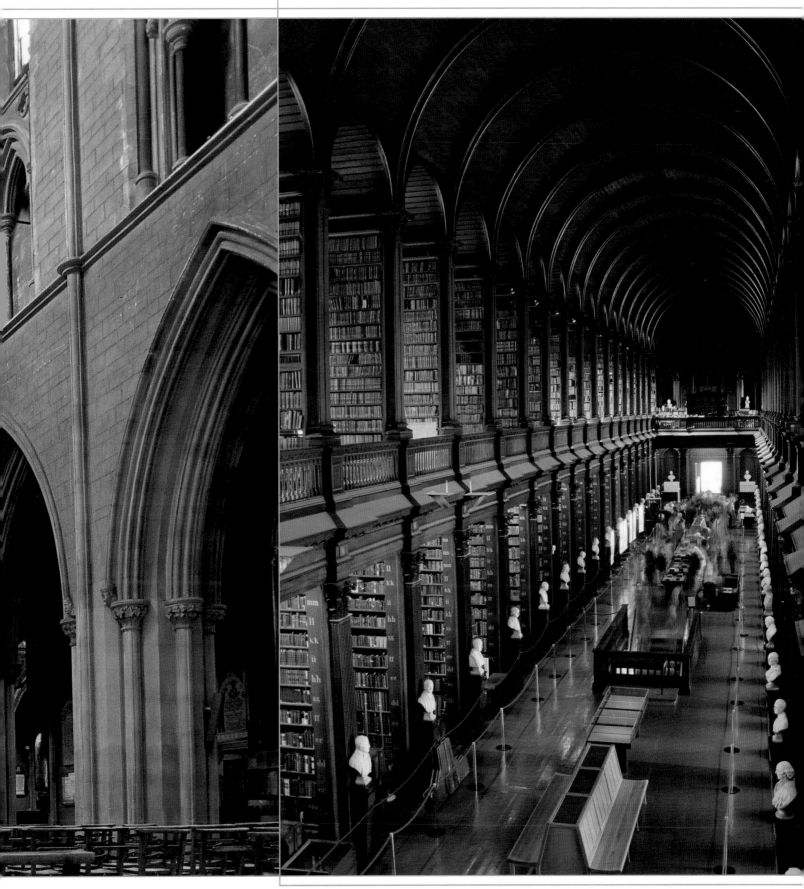

Dublin is renowned for its lively nightlife, which is unrivalled in the British Isles. Nightclubs, bars, restaurants and pubs in all styles of architecture are a main feature in many parts of the city. Traditional pubs include the old Temple Bar, the Europa and the Victorian (1895) Stag's Head. Smoking has been banned in pubs since 2004.

In Temple Bar, the "in" place for enjoying Dublin nightlife, pubs and restaurants stand cheek by jowl. The district with its old houses and narrow alleys was cleaned up in the 1980s. At the Guinness Storehouse visitor attraction in the Guinness Brewery, you can learn all about this famous dark beer, and then enjoy the panoramic views across the city from the bar on the seventh floor (right).

PUBS IN DUBLIN

In the mid-19th century, some 15,000 tavern licences were granted. Even before that taverns played a pivotal role in Irish society. In rural areas, the pub is still the heart of the village. More than just a place to drink, the pub is a gathering place, prime source of information and cultural center, providing live music, singing and dancing.

Every fifth building in Dublin is said to have been a tavern in the 17th century. Nowadays, Dubliners and visitors to the city still have a choice of at least 800 pubs for their evening's entertainment. Davy Byrne's Pub in Duke Street, which features in "Ulysses", the James Joyce novel set in Dublin on a single day, June 16th, is on the

Bloomsday commemoration route, named after Leopold Bloom, the main character in the book. The Bailey, across the road from Davy Byrne's Pub, is also mentioned, but the original building has not survived. Since so many great Irish writers are known to have had a fondness for drink, literary pub crawls have been popular with

visitors to Dublin for years. Arthur Guinness, who opened the famous brewery in Dublin in 1759, tested his unique brew of malt and roasted barley until this incomparable stout was black and bitter, yet velvety enough to ensure it would remain a popular worldwide Irish export to this day.

The lighthouse at the entrance to Howth port on the headland of the same name north of Dublin was built in 1818. The town boasts a major Irish fishing port. Built in 1804 as a defence against Napoleon, the Martello tower in Dun Laoghaire is immortalized in James Joyce's novel, "Ulysses".

At Balbriggan, a tranquil coastal town with beautiful sandy beaches, another Martello tower was built to safeguard the coast from French invasion. Ingeniously constructed inside, Martello towers were built within sight of one another to ensure a strong coastal defence.

The coast at Dublin

Dublin is flanked north and south by traditional seaside resorts such as pretty Dun Laoghaire. In the early 19th century the British government built what are known as Martello towers along the coast to defend the region from French invasion by sea. The best known Martello tower is at Sandycove, a small town beside Dun Laoghaire. In 1904, James Joyce spent a few days there and immortalized the town in "Ulysses". Now there is a small Joyce museum there. The Howth Peninsula is north of Dublin. From the ruins of St Mary's Abbey or from the coastal footpath along the cliffs, you have stunning views of Ireland's Eye, a rocky island with a ruined 8th-century church and another Martello tower. Howth Castle, probably the oldest continually inhabited house in Ireland, has been the seat of the St Lawrence family for over five centuries.

Rounded by the effect of Ice Age glaciation, the Wicklow Mountains start south of Dublin, extending southwards straight across County Wicklow for a stretch of around 60 km (37 miles). Situated on the outlying hills of the Wicklow Mountains, Powerscourt Estate is a fine old country house with grounds laid out in 1740, generally regarded as having some of the most beautiful gardens in Ireland.

The Wicklow Mountains

The loneliest stretch of country on the Irish east coast is barely an hour from Dublin. The Wicklow Way runs for 130 km (81 miles) from the sprawling suburbs of the capital straight through the mountains – across deserted moorland and bare peaks, through wooded valleys and past the country's highest waterfall. Powerscourt Waterfall, which belongs to the 18th-century Powerscourt Estate, plunging over 120 m (394 ft) into a valley. Although the highest elevation in Wicklow, Lugnaquilla, is only 926 m (3,038 ft), this is wild country, where highwaymen and rebels operated with impunity in the old days. Even now the region is sparsely settled: although Greater Dublin continues to grow, County Wicklow has a population of only about 100,000 – fewer inhabitants than it had before the Great Famine of the 1840s.

In Glendalough, the monastic site is linked with the legends that have grown up around its founder, St Kevin. A tall (33 m/108 ft) round tower and a High Cross dating from the 8th century are particularly noteworthy. As one legend has it, Kevin, a hermit, chose to sleep in an almost inaccessible cave on the Upper Lake. When he was found there by a young girl, the saint is said to have almost succumbed to her charms, but he threw her in the lake instead.

Glendalough

Ireland is full of monastic establishments in beautiful places but none is as enchanting as Glendalough, the "Valley of Two Lakes" on the eastern edge of the Wicklow Mountains. St Kevin is said to have founded the monastery there. As legend has it, the saint retreated to Glendalough in the 6th century to live as a hermit but was followed by so many disciples that he had to found a monastery. Glendalough survived several fires and attacks mounted by the Vikings, the Normans and the English (1398) before it was disbanded during the Reformation. The monastic site on the Two Lakes houses the ruins of the monastery, which include a roofed church, called "Kevin's Kitchen" because the roof is constructed like a chimney. A path leads to the Upper Lake and a cave hewn into the rock, where St Kevin is reputed to have slept.

Its isolated location protected the monastery of Clonmacnoise from attack for a long time, but in 1552 marauding English soldiers put an end to a cultural flower that had bloomed for 1,000 years.

Clonmacnoise Monastery, which was founded ca 545 by St Ciarán, was the final resting place of the kings of Connacht and Tara. In 1198, Rory O'Connor, the last High King of Ireland, was buried here.

Clonmacnoise

The unique monastic site of Clonmacnoise is situated on a bend of the River Shannon in County Offaly. In the Middle Ages, the monastery was renowned throughout Europe as a focal point for religious scholarship. The site is visited for its round tower, the remains of a cathedral and eight smaller churches, known as "temples", dating from the 11th to the 17th centuries. The largest group of Celtic High Crosses in Ireland is a highlight. To protect them from wind and weather, the most precious crosses, dating from the first millennium, have been removed to a visitor complex, which presents the history of the site. A visit to the National Museum in Dublin, where the books and liturgical treasures from Clonmacnoise are on display, is a must for anyone who wants to fully appreciate the achievements of this monastic culture.

Two of Ireland's most famous ruined monastic sites are near Kilkenny: Kells Priory, a vast Augustinian establishment, and Jerpoint Abbey, a Cistercian foundation, both of which date from the 12th century. Famous

Kilkenny Castle, until very recently the seat of the Butler family, is in the town of Kilkenny. Three round towers remain from the original castle; the other buildings date from much later.

Kilkenny

The round tower on the hill by the cathedral affords the best views of the pretty town of Kilkenny, much visited for its medieval buildings, of which it boasts more than any other Irish city. Monks and nobles had lived here for more than 1,000 years but the heyday of Kilkenny dates from the late 12th century, when the Norman Castle was built. Enacted in 1366, the Statutes of Kilkenny prohibited marriages between English settlers and the indigenous Irish as well as the use of the Irish language. In 1391, the Butlers of Ormonde acquired the Castle and remained loyal to the English crown in the 17th century. In 1967, a member of the Butler family, the 6th Marquess and 24th Earl of Ormonde, sold the castle to the Castle Restoration Committee. Several state rooms are now open to the public. Generations of Butlers are buried in the Gothic cathedral.

About 70 per cent of Irish land is devoted to agriculture, much of it to pasture. Dairy cows and beef cattle, poultry, pigs and sheep are raised here. A popular breed is the Suffolk Sheep, which, as its name indicates, originally came from England.

At regularly held cattle and sheep auctions, Irish farmers keep up with developments in livestock breeding. Traditional local breeds of cattle and sheep are sold alongside new-breed high producers imported from the European continent.

FARMING

Ireland lives up to its image as the "Emerald Isle", which was once in large part owing to its being an agricultural economy. Today the economic focus has shifted somewhat. Agriculture in Ireland today mainly means pasture rather than arable land and livestock breeding. Ireland's entry into the EU in 1973 proved a blessing for large landowners especially and led to the introduction of intensive agriculture in many sectors of farming. For instance, sheep subsidies from Brussels have led to a steady growth in the ovine population. At 4.5 million, at one time it surpassed the human population. Although overgrazing in many areas has been the consequence, sheep are still omnipresent in rural Ireland. Geological factors and climatic conditions have affected Irish agriculture in various ways. On the one hand, the mild Atlantic winters and high precipitation rates are good for crop growth. On the other, large parts of the country are unproductive blanket bog. Dairy products and meat come from the fertile regions of the south and east. Mixed farming, involving both the production of crops and livestock farming, is still sufficiently common to sustain the image of an agrarian economy and rural way of life that is close to nature, in spite of a huge increase in industrial exports.

The ruins of Dunbrody Abbey, founded in the 12th century in the south-west of County Wexford, are a testament to Cistercian architecture at its best. This richly ornate and vibrant Celtic High Cross stands in the Irish National Heritage Park, a spacious open-air museum near the city of Wexford.

Built in the latter half of the 19th century, in the elaborate Neo-Gothic style, Johnstown Castle is outside the Wexford city limits. The castle incorporates part of an old Norman stronghold. The gardens, with 200 different species of flora, are well worth a visit.

Wexford

County Wexford does not have the rugged scenery of other Irish regions but it does boast beautiful sandy beaches. The region between the Blackstairs Mountains and the sea enjoys more hours of sunshine and less precipitation than anywhere else on the island. Sea links to other countries are short from here so cultural influences from abroad are more noticeable than elsewhere in Ireland. Once a port city, Wexford was founded by the Vikings. In the Middle Ages settlers arrived from Wales, forming an ethnic group that spoke its own language into the 19th century. Ferries from France and Wales dock at Rosslare instead of Wexford because the port there has silted up, making it no longer suitable for passenger and shipping lines. The city of Wexford is now known internationally for its opera festival, held annually in October.

One of the best scenic stopping points in the region is the Ladies' View at Killarney: Queen Victoria enjoyed this superlative view of the Upper Lake on a visit to the lakes of Killarney in 1861 – hence the name.

The Dingle Peninsula is stunningly beautiful, with wild romantic coastal scenery (small picture). Middle: Mount Brandon, veiled in cloud, and on the left, behind it, the "Three Sisters" cliffs on the steep coast.

MUNSTER

Idyllic coastlines, picture-book villages and romantic lake country, steep cliffs and legendary islands, testimonials to ancient civilisation, cities steeped in history and pulsating urban areas are all found in Ireland's largest province. Munster (Irish: Mumhan) is situated in the south-west of Ireland and comprises six counties: Clare, Cork, Kerry, Limerick, Tipperary and Waterford. The name of the province is thought to derive from that of the Celtic goddess Muma.

The limestone landscape of the Burren boasts bizarre rock formations (right-hand page). In spring it is covered with enchanting flowers (left to right): Marsh Orchid, Silver Thistle, Pyramidal Orchid, Common Primrose and Hypericum. Below: Poulnabrone Dolmen, with its tabular capstone.

The Burren

An English officer, who went with Cromwell's army to the karst country of County Clare, had no eye for its haunting beauty. He found "not enough water to drown a man, trees to hang one, nor earth to bury him". The vast (250 sq km/96.53 sq miles) limestone plateau is called "The Burren" (great rock) and only at first sight does it appear bleak and grey. In spring, lush seams of flowers thrive in cracks in the rocks: a medley of Alpine, Mediterranean and Arctic species. Saxifrage and several species of orchid are found here. In addition, signs of prehistoric human habitation abound on the Burren: more than 60 megalithic tombs and some 500 Neolithic and Iron Age ring forts indicate that the Burren was anything but deserted. An impressive monument is the Poulnabrone Dolmen, a once earth-covered portal tomb (ca 3000 BC).

Spectacular coastal scenery south of Galway Bay: the famous Cliffs of Moher. In the north, at O'Brien's Tower, the sheer cliffs rise some 200 m/656 ft from the Atlantic; to the south they are lower (120 m/ 394 ft). Europe's highest sheer cliffs, stretch for 8 km (5 miles). Nesting sea-birds throng the nooks and crannies in the cliffs: black-legged kittiwakes, common guillemots and Atlantic puffins.

The Cliffs of Moher

Between Liscannor and Doolin the coastal panorama is dramatic, with towering cliffs (up to 200 m/656 ft). Walkers rejoice in a long (35 km/22 miles) stretch of scenic coastal footpath. Looking from the dizzying heights of the Cliffs of Moher at the spray and foam lashing eroded sea stacks far below, you have some idea of the power of the Atlantic breakers. The southern end of the long cliffs at Hag's Head is an ideal place for experiencing the Atlantic light. It is an awe-inspiring spectacle at sunset, when the rays of the sun shining through clouds on the horizon, "the majesty that shuts his burning eye", tint the layers of sandstone and slate. Liscannor is known for the allegedly miraculous powers of the water in Brigid's Well. Small but much frequented, Doolin is famous worldwide for the traditional music festival hosted by its three pubs.

Coastal regions have always had to defend themselves from raids launched from the sea: County Clare is no exception, as Doona-gore Castle, a 16th-century fortified tower house, shows. Lighthouses such as Loop Head serve modern seafarers. Kilkee is a Victorian seaside resort town with a beautiful, long sandy beach fringing a horseshoe bay: the perfect invitation to take long walks around the bay. Towards the west, there are some impressive rock formations, which are dwarfed by Lookout Hill (60 m/197 ft).

The Clare coast

Visitors throng to Clare, the "singing county", and not just for the good traditional music in the pubs. The fine coastal scenery, with cliffs and beautiful sandy beaches, make Clare ideal for water sports and family holidays. The Loop Head headland points like a long finger into the sea towards the west. On the north side, Kilkee is the most popular resort town, with a spotlessly clean beach protected from the Atlantic storms by the Duggerna Reef, so the swimming is safe here. At low tide small pools teem with crustaceans and small fish veiled in delicate filaments of seaweed. The mouth of the River Shannon forms the south side of the Loop Head peninsula. Boats go from Kilrush to take visitors out to see the dolphins in the Shannon Estuary and Scattery Island, no longer inhabited but dotted with monastic ruins.

Today, the heart of Limerick is south-west of Irish Town. The city 's heart is O'Connell Street with its beautifully restored Georgian houses and a monument to Daniel O'Connell, champion of Catholic Emancipation and Home Rule.

King John's Castle on the River Shannon in Limerick is the largest Anglo-Norman fort in Ireland (completed in 1210). It is surprisingly well preserved with an imposing keep, three round towers and a gatehouse with two towers.

Limerick

Limerick (population 91,000) is the third largest city in the Republic of Ireland. The prolonged Irish economic miracle has spruced up this city on the Shannon so that it looks a lot more inviting than it did a generation ago. Limerick found it hard to shed its reputation as a poor industrial city. King John's Castle and Protestant St Mary's Cathedral are in the old English Town section. The Irish-speaking inhabitants of Limerick once had to live in Irish Town, outside the fortifications, a measure of segregation that caused resentment between the two groups. A highlight of a visit is the Hunt Museum, which houses the most important collection of medieval Irish art after the National Museum in Dublin. The superlative collections of ancient and modern art from Ireland and abroad were donated by the Hunt family. The museum opened in 1997.

Apart from King John's Castle in Limerick, there are other important castles near the city: Bunratty Castle is a picture-perfect medieval square tower house. The Bunratty Folk Park, an open-air museum at the Castle, features reconstructed early 19th-century cottages. Adare Manor, once the stately home of the Dunraven family, was converted into the Adare Manor Hotel and Golf Resort several years ago. The spacious grounds, much of which are now a golf course, contain the romantic ruins of 13th-century Desmond Castle (small picture below).

Castles in County Limerick

Limerick is surrounded by fertile pastures and meadows, territory that was once fought over by Vikings, Celts and Anglo-Normans. The Vikings had a trading post in the grounds of Bunratty Castle 1,000 years ago. The Anglo-Normans built a fort on the site three times but lost each one to the Irish clans. The present castle is the fourth and remained in the O'Brien and MacNamara families until Cromwell's troops arrived in the 17th century. In 1954 Lord Gort bought the castle, by then dilapidated, restored it, furnished it with 15th- and 16th-century antiques from all over Europe and opened it to the public as a venue for wedding parties and medieval banquets. At pretty Adare nearby, the Earl of Dunraven built Adare Manor (completed in 1862), now a luxury hotel and golf resort, in the Neo-Gothic style, to resemble a fairy-tale castle.

The Rock of Cashel was the seat of the Kings of Munster for centuries before the Norman invasion. The oldest building in the complex is a dry-stone round tower (28 m/92 ft). The cathedral was built between the round tower and the chapel in the 13th century. The most important building on the Rock of Cashel is the beautiful Cormac's Chapel (consecrated in 1134), a superlative example of Irish Romanesque. The chancel boasts impressive fresco fragments depicting the Baptism of Christ and a fortified city, presumably Jerusalem.

The Rock of Cashel

The Rock of Cashel, a limestone outcrop looming from the midst of a green plain in County Tipperary, was pre-destined to importance because of its excellent strategic location. As the legend goes, the rock fell from the Devil's mouth one day while he was flying over the site and caught sight of St Patrick. This is where Patrick is supposed to have made the shamrock the national symbol of Ireland by using its three leaves to explain the mystery of the Holy Trinity. The earliest buildings on the Rock of Cashel, a round tower and Cormac's Chapel, date from the 12th and 13th centuries. The cathedral was erected when the chapel became too small to hold the congregation. The 15th-century Hall of the Vicars Choral, in which an old St Patrick's Cross is kept, was built for the vicars choral, laymen (minor canons etc) appointed to assist in the chanting at mass.

Dingle, the northernmost peninsula in County Kerry boasts grandiose, albeit bare scenery. The landscape is particularly impressive in autumn, when the sea vents its wrath on the land – on this stranded ship at Slea Head or in the booming surf off Great Blasket Island. Dingle (An Daingean) on the south side of the peninsula is a particularly charming town with brightly painted houses. Once an important base for trade, Dingle now lives entirely from tourism. West of Dingle is a Gaeltacht area, where Irish is the language spoken in homes.

The Dingle Peninsula

The Dingle Peninsula is the most northerly of five peninsulas in County Kerry, pointing west like fingers. With its mountains, rocky coast and beautiful beaches, the Dingle Peninsula boasts some of Ireland's most beautiful scenery. The mountains flanking the Connor Pass, the highest (456 m/1,496 ft) in Ireland, are a paradise for hill-walkers, while surfers find excellent conditions on the Inch headland (5 km/3.11 miles long) on the south side of the Dingle Peninsula. As is the case everywhere else in western Ireland, Dingle has Early Christian sites, including the "beehive cells" once inhabited by hermits. As the legend has it, Brandon, the patron saint of Kerry, prayed on Mount Brandon before setting out for America in the early 6th century in his flimsy coracle (currach), a wicker boat covered with animal hides, with a company of 14 monks.

Irish monks sought out Skellig Michael, the larger of the two Skellig islands, as a refuge in the 6th century, but the Vikings also found it later. Each hermit lived in a large beehive cell of dry-stone masonry. The only way to explore Skellig Michael is by foot. Little Skellig, the smaller of the two Skelligs, has always been uninhabited and is now a bird sanctuary: gannets and Atlantic puffins nest in their thousands on the rocks here.

The Skelligs

George Bernard Shaw once said that the Skelligs belonged to the realm of dreams. It is not easy to reach Skellig Michael, the larger of the two Skelligs. The crossing is possible only in good weather. If a storm blows up, you may have to stay on the island until the sea calms down again. The hazardous passage does not deter thousands of visitors annually from landing on the island to wear down the 650 stone steps leading up to the 6th-century monastery, which, judging by the name of the island, must have been consecrated to St Michael. The fascinating site includes the ruins of a 12th-century church, gravestones and a well. The monks' cells are particularly intriguing: dry-stone beehive structures like trulli. As legend has it, St Patrick banished poisonous snakes from Ireland, hurling the last of them into the sea from the cliffs of Skellig with the Archangel's help.

The "Ring of Kerry", the tourist route round the Iveragh Peninsula, covers some of the most stunning scenery in all western Europe. Kenmare Bay (usually called the Kenmare River) extends between the Iveragh Peninsula and Beara. The countryside is dotted with cottages.

About 4 km (2.5 miles) from the south coast of Iveragh is Staigue stone fort, an Iron Age ring fort about 2,000 years old, which was probably a defensive fort used by local kings. It is one of the best preserved dry-stone monuments of this type in Ireland.

The south coast of Iveragh

Following the coastline most of the way, the "Ring of Kerry" (170 km/106 miles) route round the Iveragh Peninsula is definitely a high point of any trip to Ireland. The changing vistas of mountains and bays are breathtaking. This spectacular trip is not just scenic; it also includes cultural highlights, such as the Staigue stone fort, an Iron Age Celtic ringfort with walls 4 m (13 ft) thick, and Derrynane House, home of Daniel O'Connell, also known as the Liberator. A popular starting-point for the tour is Kenmare, a small picturesque town with houses in pastel shades at the head of Kenmare Bay (Kenmare River). Known worldwide for Kenmare lace, made at the 19th-century convent of the Poor Clare Sisters, the town was laid out in about 1670 by Sir William Petty, an ancestor of the first Marquess of Landsdowne.

Port Magee may be a picturesque place in many visitors' eyes, but the reality is that the lives of the local fishermen are quite hard. The locals here maintain that the houses are painted in such pretty shades to help them find their way home after a night out at the pub.

The west coat of Iveragh is famous for its scenic grandeur: Puffin Island in Puffin Sound off St Finan is thronged with nesting Atlantic Puffins and gannets. If you are looking for solitude, head for the Ballinskelligs in the bay or to the active Cromwell Point lighthouse.

The west coast of Iveragh

In the south-west of the Iveragh Peninsula is Caherciveen, once home to the most popular hero of more recent Irish history: Daniel O'Connell. A barrister who inherited a fortune made by his family through trade and smuggling, O'Connell was free to devote himself in the British parliament to the repeal of anti-Catholic legislation. The limited Catholic Emancipation Act of 1829 was largely his doing. An excursion to Valentia Island is well worth taking: linked to the mainland by a bridge, the island boasts Europe's most westerly port. The first commercially viable undersea telegraph cable linking Europe and Canada was laid from here (attempted from 1857, finally successful in 1866). The Skellig Experience Heritage Centre, which provides a wealth of information on the life led by the monks on Skellig Michael, is also located on the island.

Ross Castle, which dates from the late 15th century, stands on a headland jutting into Lough Leane, the largest of the three Lakes of Killarney. It is linked with Muckross Lake and Upper Lake by a waterway.

South-west of the city of Killarney is the Killarney National Park, an attractive area with three large lakes, the Lakes of Killarney. Upper Lake, the smallest, is more remote and is ideal for freshwater angling.

Killarney National Park

Killarney National Park (102.89 sq km/25,435 acres) near Killarney encompasses mountains and three lakes formed by Ice-Age glaciation. As a national park, the region is off-limits for cars. Take a horse-drawn jaunting car through the Gap of Dunloe, a gorge in the shadow of Purple Mountain, aptly named after the shades of the heather that blooms on it in late summer. A much more strenuous undertaking is climbing Carrauntoohil (1,038 m/3,406 ft), Ireland's highest mountain. The oaks growing in Killarney National Park are unusual because most trees were felled centuries ago and the yew wood is a botanical rarity. There are only two others like it in Europe. The Strawberry Tree is often encountered in Ireland. Native to the Mediterranean, the Strawberry Tree grows quite tall and bears inedible red fruits, hence the name.

As well as saltwater fishing, freshwater angling is a popular sport in Ireland. A wealth of rivers, streams and lakes make Ireland Europe's best destination for an angling holiday: trout and good coarse fishing (tench, pike, roach) in beautiful scenery. Fishing close to the coast in small boats used to provide farmers with winter income. This form of fishing is dying out.

FISHING

Although the seas round Ireland teem with many species of fish, commercial sea fishing has played an important economic role in Ireland only since the Second World War. Since then the Irish fisheries have been built up and regulated responsibly by regional fisheries boards. Modern trawlers operate on a commercial scale out of the ports of Killybegs in Donegal und Castletownbere in Cork. Processing plants, in turn, provide many jobs on land. The Irish boats have to contend with stiff competition from well equipped European factory ships, from Spain, particularly. Despite the general overfishing of the Atlantic waters, however, the Irish west coast is, at least compared with the North Sea, still healthy and relatively unpolluted, which makes Irish fish and crustaceans sought after by gourmets. Atlantic salmon, scallops, oysters and mussels are cultivated at specialized fish farms in a highly viable industry – mainly for export but also for the increasing number of excellent seafood restaurants opening everywhere in Ireland. Irish trawlers catch haddock, mackerel, plaice and several kinds of white fish as well as such delicacies as Dover sole and monkfish. Closer to shore, small boats put out from the many picturesque fishing ports along this part of the coast to catch lobster, crab and prawns.

Typical of the west of the peninsula are tiny inlets that are still unspoiled by tourism. Small fishing ports and remote villages exemplify the untouched scenery in this region.

An idyllic setting: Garnish Bay with Dursey Island on the west side of the Beara Peninsula. Northern gannets and other seabirds find this official sanctuary an ideal habitat.

Garnish Bay

The deck of a yacht may be the best vantage point for experiencing the serene beauty of the many tiny inlets in the far west of the Beara Peninsula. On your trip you're likely to see seals basking in the sun on rocks rising up out of the sea. Garnish Bay is south of Allihies, in a region in which copper ore was mined until the 1930s. Aficionados of long, solitary walks are in the perfect place for them along this stretch of the Irish coast and on Dursey Island, which is linked with the mainland by Europe's only cable car over water across the dangerous waters of Dursey Sound – no boat crosses the sound. There is only a handful of houses on the island – no pubs, no shops and no overnight accommodation. Walkers are accompanied only by the cries of gulls and the pounding of the surf on the high cliffs, and are rewarded by the panoramic views.

Less well-known to visitors than the Ring of Kerry, the Ring of Beara is no less spectacular. The interior of the Beara Peninsula is a country of mountains and small lakes – as here at Healy Pass with Glenmore Lake or at Lauragh (below, right). The tiny coastal village of Eyeries, which still has little tourist infrastructure, is said to be the most distinctive in all Ireland. The terraces in this pretty village look to be straight out of the paintbox (even the church is bright yellow).

The Ring of Beara

Providing spectacular vistas of mountains and the sea, the narrow road round the rocky Beara Peninsula runs for 140 km (87 miles). Weather permitting, you can see as far as County Kerry. Beara was the clan region of the O'Sullivan Bere, who lived at Dunboy Castle near Castletownbere. When English troops took the castle in 1602, 1,000 clan members who had not been involved in the siege set out through Ireland to distant County Leitrim. Only 35 of them made it. Waves of emigration continued to reduce the population of Beara; it is still sparsely settled and without major towns. The ruins of a Victorian stately home known as Puxley's Castle on the bay at Castletownbere was home to the owner of the Beara copper mines. In 1920 the Irish Republican Army burnt the house down in retaliation for the destruction by Crown forces of many houses sheltering IRA men.

The coastal scenery of the Beara Peninsula is magnificently wild and extremely varied: distant mountains loom high over blue bays, with green pastures and pretty little fishing villages set in between – a view of Ballydonegan Bay at Allihies. Holding their own on the Beara Peninsula coast: traditional Irish cottages. For centuries they have remained unchanged: rectangular ground-plan, one-storeyed and thatched. Many of them have been restored and turned into self-catering holiday lets.

The coast of the Beara Peninsula

Glengarriff, on the south side of the Beara Peninsula, was a resort popular even in the Victorian era for its mild climate. Over a century ago, the owners of Garnish Island took advantage of the warm winters to turn a barren stony spot into a lush garden. Boatloads of topsoil were brought to the island to transform it into a paradise of subtropical plants blooming from April to September. An avenue of vast Eucalyptus trees leads to one of Ireland's oldest "castle" hotels, now the Glengarriff Eccles Hotel, on Bantry Bay. In calm weather this coast looks idyllic but its appearance is deceptive. Hidden reefs and treacherous currents make the seas around the peninsula a ship graveyard, full of the wrecks of English battleships and Spanish men-of-war, trading vessels from America and Europe and the boats of local fishermen and smugglers.

Despite what some Europeans think: only three per cent of the Irish have red hair and they are not just of Celtic descent – remember the Vikings. Nor are there few Irish in the world: 40 million US citizens are proud of ancestors from the Emerald Isle.

THE IRISH

Some have red hair, many more are dark-haired and some are golden blond. The Irish are known for a love of drink and their charm is proverbial. The Irish are hospitable, innovative and love music and story-telling. Thus the clichés. The population of Ireland is only five million but the country's image is huge. Ireland punches way above its weight in producing so many world-class writers in English. From 500 BC, Celts mingled with a native substrate to become the dominant ethnic group. From the 9th century, the Vikings inhabited large coastal areas until the Battle of Clontarf in 1014, when most fled. By 1170, the English crown was ruling Ireland and many Anglo-Normans never left. The 17th century saw a decisive break. The power of the Irish nobles was broken and King James V of Scotland and I of England settled Scottish and English soldiers in Ireland to secure England against Spanish and Portuguese attack. Those "plantations" caused the profound religious and ethnic schism within Ulster, where the descendants of the Protestant settlers live. The complex ethnic background of the Irish has made the country uniquely culturally vibrant. Only about two per cent of the population speak Irish at home but tradition lives on in Irish folk music as well as Irish sports such as hurling and Gaelic football.

The sea with its infinite moods and faces is fascinating here: from soft sandy beaches to steep cliffs; here at Barley Cove Beach. The lighthouse at Fastnet Rock is in an even more spectacular setting. In 1796, the White family of Bantry House betrayed an Irish-led invasion by a French fleet to the British government, which gratefully rewarded the Whites with a baronetcy for their loyalty.

Bantry Bay and Mizen Head

The great house of the Earls of Bantry, now with bed-and-breakfast accommodation and with its grounds open to the public, is full of beautiful things, but the spectacular view of Bantry Bay from this stately home was its owners' greatest treasure. Many of the magnificent furnishings and works of art were collected in the 19th century by the second Earl on trips to the Continent. Sheep's Head, the more northerly of the two peninsulas, is virtually uninhabited. Mizen Head, the most south-westerly point of Ireland, is often visited, especially for the dual attractions at its tip. Barley Cove has a superlative sandy beach with protected areas for safe swimming but further on there are reliably big waves that are really appreciatd by surfers. Built in 1910, Mizen Head Lighthouse is a popular destination with walkers along the beach but is no longer manned.

The history of Cork began when St Finbarr founded a monastic settlement in the 7th century. The saint chose to build it on an island in the River Lee. The river and canals – here the South Canal – still shape the Cork cityscape. Right, back: Holy Trinity Church, built in 1832.

West of Cork the coast grows wilder and more rugged but is dotted with pretty fishing villages. Cliff walks along Sheep's Head Peninsula and to the lighthouses and the Mizen Head dolmen at Ireland's most south-westerly point reward the effort with solitude and superlative vistas.

Cork

Corkonians, the inhabitants of the second-largest city in the Republic of Ireland, have always tended to view their native city as an island metropolis – long before it was designated European Cultural Capital in 2005. Encircled by green hills, Cork is on the estuary of the River Lee and boasts one of the world's largest natural ports. Recent years have seen Cork attractively refurbished, especially along the rejuvenated Patrick Street.

Street cafés and stylish shops enliven bustling pedestrian zones. In a more old-fashioned vein, there is the English Market, built in 1842, where fresh seafood awaits buyers. Cork became prosperous in the 18th century through trade in foodstuffs, notably the export of Irish butter. The Butter Exchange near Shandon church and the Butter Museum attest to the historical status of the butter trade in the Cork economy.

In 1915, the lighthouse at the Old Head of Kinsale witnessed a maritime war atrocity: the German embassy in Washington issued warnings before a German submarine sank the Cunard liner Lusitania, taking almost 2,000 civilian lives.

Kinsale is a popular and pleasant holiday resort situated on the mouth of the River Brandon, a natural anchorage. Boats for angling and yachts are for hire here. The town is enchanting, with narrow streets and houses in pretty pastel tints.

The coast at Kinsale

The pretty port town of Kinsale on the south coast has been moulded by the sea. Both water sports aficionados and gourmets populate Kinsale in summer because the coast does not just attract yachtsmen; commercial fishing boats catch fish for excellent restaurants. A battle off Kinsale in 1601 saw the defeat of a Spanish fleet in the service of Irish aristocrats that led to the "Flight of the Earls". In the 17th century, the Stuart kings of Great Britain fortified Kinsale port. Two forts were named after them: James Fort, in ruins south-west of the town, and Charles Fort on the other side of the port where guided tours are available. South of Kinsale a sequence of headlands and bays on the Seven Heads Peninsula at Timoleague make for lovely coastal scenery that is soft and inviting and perhaps a welcome change after the rugged grandeur of the west coast.

Lismore Castle, a 12th-century keep, was rebuilt in the Gothic Revival style in the mid-19th century. Groups of affluent guests rent it when the Duke of Devonshire is not in residence.

Lismore, with Lismore Castle, is situated near the south coast on the River Blackwater and at the foot of the Knockmealdown Mountains in County Waterford.

Lismore Castle

Lismore is a small town with a great past. An abbey founded in the 7th century by St Carthage grew into an important base for scholarship despite frequent raids by marauding Vikings and, later, the Normans. The cathedral was almost destroyed by English troops in the 16th century. The new church built in 1633 recalls the glories of the past. Lismore Castle, overlooking the valley of the River Blackwater, goes back much further.

Robert Boyle, the "father of modern chemistry", was born at Lismore. In the mid-19th century, a keep seven centuries old was remodelled into a castle in the Gothic Revival style by the sixth Duke of Devonshire. The present Duke still has apartments in the castle and is often in residence. The beautiful grounds are open to the public and up to twenty-three guests can rent the castle when the Duke is away.

Ardmore has one of Ireland's most beautiful round towers (30 m/98.4 ft). Dating from the 12th century, it has six storeys. The abutting ruins of St Declan's church boast splendid 9th-century reliefs: Adam and Eve, the Judgement of Solomon and the Adoration of the Magi.

Fortifications, such as this motte-and-bailey lookout tower near Ardmore, date from the period of Norman settlement of Ireland in the 12th century. The soldiers' quarters, however, were inside the bailey, an enclosed courtyard below the tower raised on its mound of earth.

Ardmore

Ardmore, a popular resort on a headland between Ardmore Bay and Youghal Bay, has a long sandy beach. St Declan, a native of Wales, christianised the area. A precursor of St Patrick, Declan built a monastic establishment here in the early 5th century with a view of Ardmore Bay. Three old stone crosses stand on a hill at the edge of the village, marking a spring named after the saint, where pilgrims used to refresh themselves.

Modern pilgrims take the route of St Declan's Way (90 km/56 miles) between Ardmore and the Rock of Cashel, consecrated to St Patrick. A 12th-century round tower, a 13th-century ruined church and an 8th-century oratory still stand on the site of Declan's monastic establishment. Magnificent 9th-century relief carvings of Old Testament scenes were incorporated in the west façade of the later church, which is now roofless.

Waterford, the county seat of County Waterford and the oldest city in Ireland, was founded by the Vikings. It is flourishing, thanks to its port and thriving industries. The region is one of Ireland's richest.

Dunmore East, a fishing village popular with tourists, is set on the slopes at the southern end of Waterford Harbour. Before reaching Waterford by water, you pass Ballynacourty lighthouse.

Waterford

Its strategic position and protected anchorage on the River Suir have ensured that Waterford has been a maritime trading base since it was founded by the Vikings in the 9th century. The city contains several buildings from its 18th-century heyday, such as City Hall and the cathedral, along with some medieval structures. Well fortified as a Viking outpost, Waterford finally fell to the Earl of Pembroke in 1170 to 1171 and remained loyal to the Anglo-Norman crown. The 10th-century Viking fortifications in the "Viking Triangle" include Reginald's Tower on the river bank. Since the 18th century the city has been famous worldwide for Waterford crystal glass. A guided tour through a former granary, now the Waterford Museum of Treasures, starts with the magnificent gold Viking Kite Brooch (1100) and features an array of the finest Waterford crystal.

Ireland is full of prehistoric monuments. Dolmens are megalithic tombs built of standing stones topped with a capstone, forming a chamber covered by a mound of earth – although many now stand bare.

ATLAS

Ireland, Irish Éire, is one of the British Isles in the Atlantic (84,405 sq km/52,447 sq miles). Interspersed with moorland and lakes, the flat or hilly central lowlands are surrounded by low mountains and in the east by the Irish Sea. Ireland has a mild oceanic climate with cool summers, mild winters and a lot of rainfall. The island (population: just under 6 million) is divided politically into the Republic of Ireland and Northern Ireland, which is part of the United Kingdom of Great Britain and Northern Ireland.

Commercial sea fishing still plays a role in the Irish economy: the sea yields herring, cod, sea bream, haddock and shellfish, while Ireland's rivers are fished by anglers for salmon and trout.

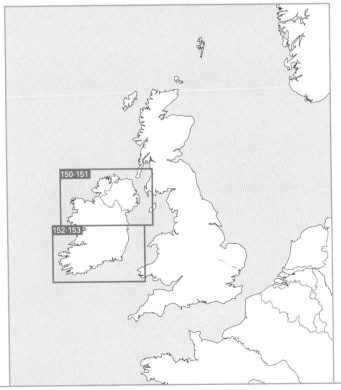

MAP KEY
1:950,000

▬▬ ┄┄	Motorway (under construction)
▬▬▬	Toll motorway
▬▬ ┄┄	4- or multi-lane road (under construction)
▬▬ ┄┄	Trunk-road (under construction)
▬▬ ┄┄	Important main road (under construction)
▬▬▬	Main road
▬▬▬	Side road
┅┅┅	Railway
▬▬▬	Restricted area
▬▬▬	National Park and nature reserve
4 **2** **A22**	Motorway number
E54	E-Road number
34 28 **N22** 66	Other street numbers
▬▬22▬▬	Motorway junction number
▬▬●▬▬	Motorway junction
🚐 ✖	Unsuitable/prohibited for caravans
🅟 ⊗	Motorway services/petrol station
⊠	Motorway services with motel
✈	Major airport
✈	Airport
✈	Airfield
⛴	Car ferry

KEY

The maps on the following pages show Ireland on a scale of 1:950,000. Geographical details have been supplemented by numerous items of useful information: the traffic and transport system has been mapped out in great detail and symbols indicate all the important sights and tourist destinations by location and type. The names of cities that tourists may find particularly interesting are highlighted in yellow. UNESCO World Natural Heritage Sites are specially marked for convenience.

SYMBOLS

Principal travel routes
- Motorway
- Railway line
- Shipping route

Remarkable landscapes and natural monuments
- UNESCO World Heritage Site (natural)
- Mountain landscape
- Ravine/canyon
- Cave
- Waterfall/rapids
- Lake country
- National Park (landscape)
- National Park (fauna)
- National Park (flora)
- National Park (culture)
- Botanical garden
- Wildlife reserve
- Whale watching
- Zoo
- Coastal landscape
- Beach
- Island

Remarkable cities and cultural monuments
- UNESCO World Heritage Site (cultural)
- Remarkable city
- Pre- and early history
- Places of Christian cultural interest
- Romanesque church
- Gothic church
- Christian monastery
- Historic cityscape
- Castle/fortress/fort
- Castle ruins
- Palace
- Technical/industrial monument
- Museum
- Space telescope
- Festivals
- Market
- Theater of war/battlefield
- Open-air museum
- Lighthouse worth seeing
- Remarkable bridge
- Windmill

Sport and leisure sites
- Golf
- Horse racing
- Sailing
- Diving
- Canoeing/rafting
- Wind surfing
- Surfing
- Seaport
- Deep-sea fishing
- Mineral/thermal spa
- Beach resort
- Amusement/theme park
- Mountain railway

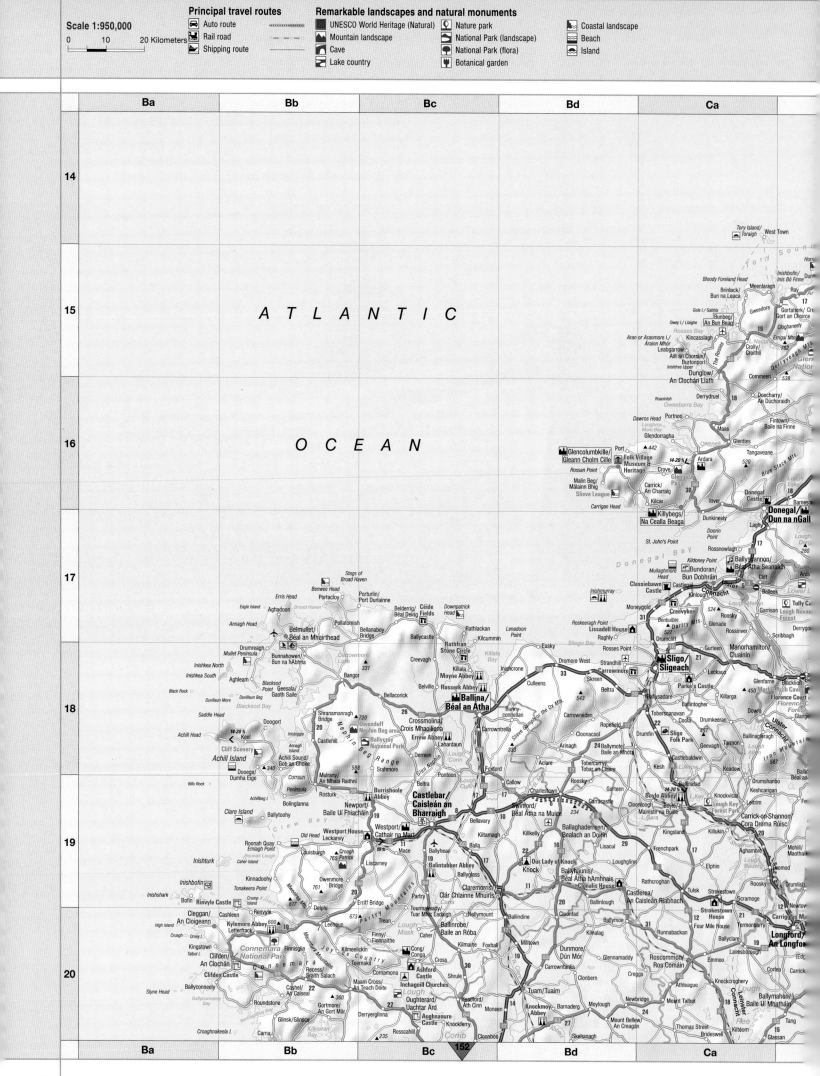

Principal travel routes

- Auto route
- Rail road
- Shipping route

Remarkable landscapes and natural monuments

- UNESCO World Heritage (Natural)
- Mountain landscape
- Cave
- Lake country
- Nature park
- National Park (landscape)
- National Park (flora)
- Botanical garden
- Coastal landscape
- Beach
- Island

	Ba	Bb	Bc	Bd	Ca

14

15

A T L A N T I C

16

O C E A N

17

Tory Island/
Toraigh   West Town

Bloody Foreland Head
Inishbofin/
Inis Bó Finne

Brinlack/
Bun na Leaca   Meenlaragh   Ray

Gola I./ Gabhla   Bunbeg/
                          An Bun Beag   Gweedore   Cloghaneely

Aran or Aranmore I./
Árainn Mhór   Kincasslagh
Leabgarrow
Inishfree Upper   Crolly/
Burtonport   Croithlí

Ailt an Chorráin
Dunglow/
An Clochán Liath

Roaninish   Derrydruel   Doocharry/
Gweebarra Bay   An Dúchoraidh   Fintown/
                                                                Baile na Finne

Dawros Head   Portnoo
Loughros
More Bay   Maas   Glenties
Glendorragha

Glencolumbkille/
Gleann Cholm Cille   Port   442   Folk Village
                              Museum &   Tangaveane
Rossan Point   Heritage   Crove

Malin Beg/   Carrick/
Málainn Bhig   An Charraig   Kilcar   Inver
Slieve League

Carrigan Head

Killybegs/
Na Cealla Beaga   Dunkineely   Donegal/
                                          Dún na nGall

St. John's Point   Doorin
                         Point

Rossnowlagh

Donegal Bay

18

19

20

Ireland

Sport and leisure destinations

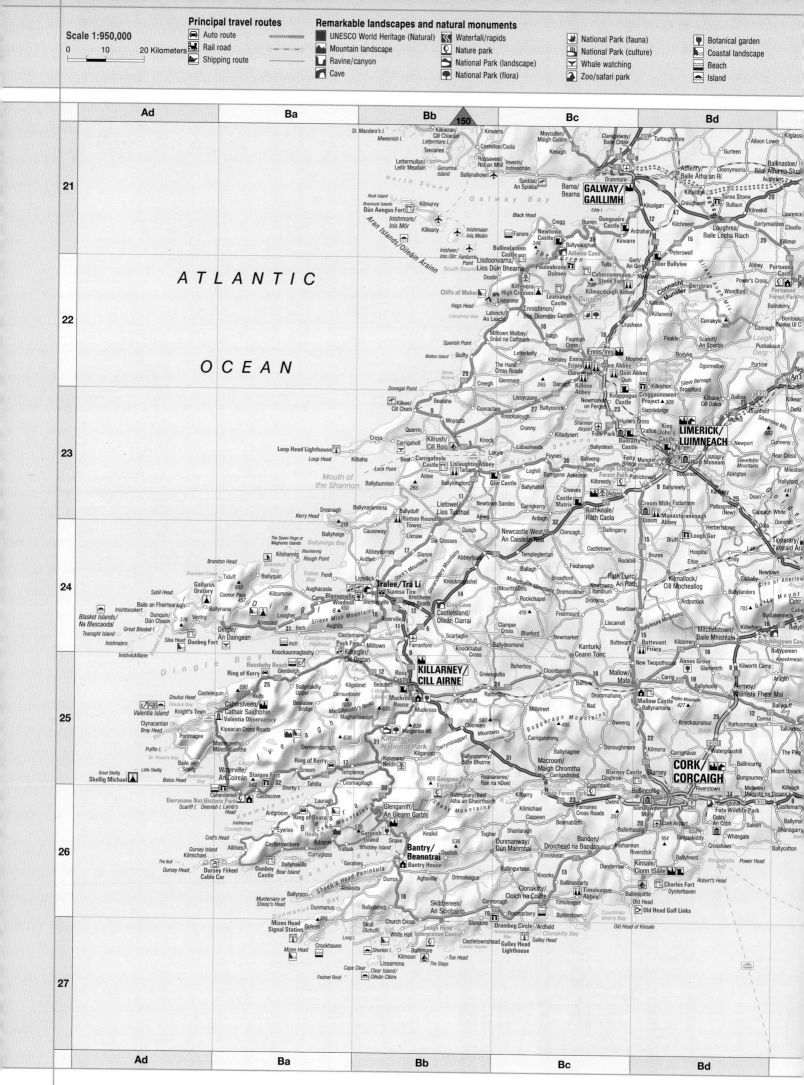

Scale 1:950,000

0   10   20 Kilometers

Principal travel routes
- Auto route
- Rail road
- Shipping route

Remarkable landscapes and natural monuments
- UNESCO World Heritage (Natural)
- Mountain landscape
- Ravine/canyon
- Cave
- Waterfall/rapids
- Nature park
- National Park (landscape)
- National Park (flora)
- National Park (fauna)
- National Park (culture)
- Whale watching
- Zoo/safari park
- Botanical garden
- Coastal landscape
- Beach
- Island

	Ad	Ba	Bb	Bc	Bd

21

St. Macdara's I.
Cill Chiaráin
Kilkieran
Mweenish I.
Lettermore I.
Teeranea
Kinvarra
Costelloe/Casla
Moycullen/
Maigh Cuilinn
Claregalway/
Baile Chláir
Turloughmore
Alloon Lower
Kilglass

Lettermullan/
Leitir Meallán
Gorumna
Island
Ballynahown
Inverin/
Indreabhán
Spiddal/
An Spidéal
Barna/
Bearna
Oranmore
**GALWAY/
GAILLIMH**
Kilcolgan
Craughwell
Athenry/
Baile Átha an Rí
Cloonymorris
Aughrim
Ballinasloe/
Béal Átha na Slua

North Sound
Galway Bay
Black Head
Cregg
Burren
Dunguaire
Castle
Ardrahan
Kinvarra
Kilchreest
Loughrea/
Baile Locha Riach
Gortymadden
Clonfe
Killimor

Rock Island
Kilmurvy
Inishmore/
Inis Mór
Killeany
Inishmaan/
Inis Meáin
Fanore
Newtown
Castle
Ballyvaughan
Burren
Aillwee Cave
Gort/
An Gort
Moor Ballylee
Petersvell
Power's Cross
Derrybrien
Woodford
Portumna
Castl
Portum
Forest Park

Brannock Islands
Dún Aengus Fort
Inisheer/
Inis Oírr
Fardurris
Point
Ballinalacken
Castle
Lisdoonvarna
Lios Dúin Bhearna
Doolin
Poulnabrone
Dolmen
Cahercommaun
Stone Fort
Kilmacduagh Abbey
Newtown
Corrakyle
Connagh
Buiros Uí C
Balinderry

South Sound
Cliffs of Moher
Hags Head
Kilfenora
High Crosses
Liscannor
Ennistimon/
Inis Díomáin
Corofin
Leamaneh
Castle
Killeen
Munster
Connacht
Lough
Cutra
Killena
Killanena
Connagh
Borrisoka
Puckaun
An t

22

Lahinch/
An Leach
Liscannor Bay
Milltown Malbay/
Sráid na Cathrach
Inagh
Fountain
Cross
Letterkelly
Crusheen
Feakle
Scariff/
An Scairbh
Corrakyle
Lough
Derg
Portroe

Spanish Point
Mutton Island
Quilty
White
Strand
The Hand
Cross Roads
Kilmaley
Ennis/
Inis
Clare Abbey
Quin Abbey
Quin
Bodyke
Ogonnelloe
An t

Donegal Point
Creegh
Glenmore
265
Darragh
Killone
Abbey
Kilkishen
Slieve Bernagh
Broadford
Killaloe/
Cill Dalua
Ballina

Kilkee/
Cill Chaoi
Bealaha
Lissycasey
Ballycorick
Newmarket
on Fergus
Knappogue
Castle
Craggaunowen
Project 309
Sixmilebridge
Kilmore
Dolla

23

Loop Head Lighthouse
Loop Head
Mouth of
the Shannon
Kilbaha
Cross
Carrigaholt
Moyasta
Cooraclare
Knockalough
Cranny
Killadysert
Shannon
Airport
Folk Park
Hurlers Cross
Cratloe
King
John's
Castle
**LIMERICK/
LUIMNEACH**
Silvermine Mts.
693
Bushfield
Kilkear

Kilrush/
Cill Rois
Beal
Carrigafoyle
Castle
Lakyle
Knock
Labasheeda
Foynes
Ballyven-
land
Bunratty
Castle
Parteen
Mungret
Newport
Cureeny
Rear Cross

Leck Point
Ballybunnion
Astee
Ballylongford
Lislaughtin Abbey
Tarbert
Glin
Glin Castle
Ballyhahill
Loghill
Barrigone
Askeaton
Kilbreedy
Patrickswell
Ballyneety
Abington
Hollyford
441

Kerry Head
Dreenagh
Ballyheige
Ballynaskreena
Ballyduff
Rattoo Round
Tower
Listowel/
Lios Tuathail
Newtown Sandes
Carrigkerry
Ardagh
Rathkeale/
Ráth Caola
Castle
Matrix
Creeves
Adare
Croom Mills
Fedamore
Kilfinny
Doon
Milestow

24

The Seven Hogs or
Maghare Islands
218
Causeway
Lixnaw
Athea
Newcastle West/
An Caisleán Nua
Cloncagh
Ballingarry
Croom
Monasteranenagh
Abbey
Herbertstown
25
Cappagh White
Donohil

Brandon Head
Brandon
Bay
Rough Point
Abbeydorney
Glanoe
Duagh
Six Crosses
Templeglantan
Feohanagh
Broadford
Rath Luirc/
An Ráth
Bruff
Lough Gur
Latin
Emly
Tipperary/
Tiobraid Ára

Brandon Creek
Tiduff
Fenit
Abbeyfeale
Ballagh
Castletown
Rockhill
Elton
Newtown
Kilmallock/
Cill Mocheallog
Kilbeheny
Gally
Mount
Aher

Gallarus
Oratory
950
Connor Pass
457
Ballyquin
Tralee
Bay
Listellick
Blennerville
Tralee/Trá Lí
Siamsa Tíre
Knocken
Cross Roads
Knocknagoshel
Mount
Collins
Dromcolliher
Dromina
Ardpatrick
785
Ballylanders
Mitchelstown
Caves
Cahir

Sybil Head
Inishtooskert
Dunquin/
Dún Chaoin
516
Kilcummin
Camp
Blennerville
Windmill
850
Crag Cave
Castleisland/
Oileán Ciarraí
Clamper
Cross
Freemount
Liscarroll
Buttevant
Kildorrery
Boolakennedy
Cahir

Blasket Islands/
Na Blascaodaí
Tearaght Island
Great Blasket I.
Anascaul
31 Inch
Slieve Mish Mountains
Aughils
Riverville
410
Newmarket
Kanturk/
Ceann Toirc
Ballyhoura Mountains
Mitchelstown/
Baile Mhistéala
Ballyporeen
Knockmeale

25

Inishvickillane
Ventry
Dingle/
An Daingean
Dunbeg Fort
Slea Head
Inch
Castlemaine
Harbour
Castlemaine
Milltown
Farranfore
Scartaglin
Knocknabul
Cross
Ballydesmond
Buttevant
Friary
New Twopothouse
Anne's Grove
Glanworth
Kilworth Camp
Araglin

Dingle Bay
Knockaunnaglashy
Killorglin/
Cill Orglan
Puck Fair
Ross
Castle
**KILLARNEY/
CILL AIRNE**
Gneevgullia
Boherboy
Cloonbannin
Mallow/
Mala
Carrig
Ballyhooly
Fermoy/
Mainistir Fhear Maí
Ballyduff

Rossbehy Beach
Glenbeigh
Ballymakilly
Upper
Beaufort
Muckross
House
Rathmore
Nad
Millstreet
Bweeng
Mallow Castle
Ballynamona
Rathcormack
Conna
Tallowbrid

Castlequin
690
Kells
Carrauntoohil
1038
MacGillycuddy's Reeks
835
Muckross
Barraduff
Drommahane
Knockaunalour
Carriganimmy
Bweeng
22
Watergrasshill
The Pike

Cahersiveen/
Cathair Saidhbhín
Bealalaw
Bridge
Maghanlawaun
580
Clonkeen
Mountains
Boggeragh Mountains
495
Donoughmore
Kilmona
Carrignavar
Glounthaune
Mount Uniack

Valentia
Observatory
Valentia
Island
Knight's Town
Kipeacan Cross Roads
638
Mangerton Mt.
838
Derrynasaggart
Macroom/
Maigh Chromtha
Carrigadrohid
Coachford
Blarney Castle
Blarney
**CORK/
CORCAIGH**
Dungourney
Midleton/
Mainistir na Corann

Clynacantan
Bray Head
Portmagee
Mastergeehy/
Máistir Gaoithe
Derreendarragh
Killarney
National Park
Kilgarvan
Ballyvourney/
Baile Bhuirne
Reananeree/
Rae na nDoirí
Carrigadrohid
Cloghroe
Ballincollig
Riverstown
Cobh/
An Cóbh
Saleen

26

Puffin I.
St. Finan's Bay
Baile an
Sceilg
Waterville/
An Coireán
Lough Currane
Ring of Kerry
Sneem
Templenoe
Kenmare/
Neidín
Kilgarvan
Roughty
Inchigeelagh
Ballingeary/
Béal Átha an Ghaorthaidh
Gougane Barra
Forest Park
605
Kilmichael
Farnanes
Cross Roads
Ovens
Gunpowder
Mills
Cork Airport
Fota Wildlife Park
Ringaskiddy
Whitegate
Shanagarry

Great Skellig
Little Skellig
Skellig Michael
Bolus Head
Staigue Fort
543
Tahilla
Coomnagillagh
Shehy Mountains
Kealkil
Shanlaragh
Bandon/
Droicheadna Bandon
Innishannon
Riverstick
Kinsale/
Cionn tSáile
Ballyfeard
Ballycotton

Derrynane Nat. Historic Park
Scariff I.
Deenish I.
Lamb's
Head
Caherdaniel
Laragh
Castlecove
Glengarriff/
An Gleann Garbh
575
Garinish
Island
Snave
Togher
Dunmanway/
Dún Mánmhaí
Enniskeane
Dunderrow
164
Crosshaven

Dursey Island
Kilmichael
The Bull
Dursey Firkeel
Cable Car
Dunboy
Castle
Bear Island
Allihies
Castletownbere
Adrigole
Healy Pass
Trafrask
Whiddy Island
**Bantry/
Beanntraí**
Bantry House
Kealkil
536
Deelish
Ballinadee
Clonakilty/
Cloich na Coillte
Timoleague
Abbey
Ballinspittle
Old Head
Charles Fort
Oysterhaven
Robert's Head
Power Head

27

Cod's Head
Coulagh Bay
Eyeries
Ballynakilla
Bere Island
Curryglass
Gerahies
Sheep's Head Peninsula
Durrus
Aghaville
Drimoleague
Connonagh
Rosscarbery
Clonakilty Bay
Galley Head
Lighthouse
Old Head of Kinsale

Muntervary or
Sheep's Head
Dunmanus
Ballyroon
Ahakista
Dunmanus
Bay
Ballydehob
Skibbereen/
An Sciobairín
Drombeg
Circle
Ardfield
Courtmac-
sherry Bay

Mizen Head
Signal Station
Goleen
Crookhaven
Mizen Head
Skull/
(Schull)
Church Cross
White Hall
Lough Hyne
Interpretive Centre
Castletownshead
Galley Head
The Stags
Glandore
Butlerstown

Cape Clear
Fastnet Rock
Long I.
Sherkin I.
Baltimore
Kilmoon
Lissamona
Clear Island/
Oileán Cléire
Roaringwater Bay
Castle Haven
Toe Head

The entries in the index refer to the main text and the maps. Each index entry is followed by a symbol (explained on p.149), which indicates the type of sight referred to. The symbol is followed by a page reference to the main text. Finally, there are details of websites that will provide up-to-date information on the places of interest and the various sights described in this book. Most of the places described in the main text will also be found in the map section, which provides a wealth of further information for visitors.

From left to right: The Clonmacnoise stone crosses; a scenic vista in Connemara; view of Dublin by night; the ruins of Dunluce Castle.

Castle Ward 🏛	151 Db18		www.nationaltrust.org.uk
			www.fjiordlands.org/strngfrd/cward.htm
Castlebar ☐ 🏛	150 Bc19		www.mayo-ireland.ie/Mayo/Towns/CasBar/CasBar.htm
			www.life-spa.ie/lspa/www/index.asp
			www.castlebar.ie
Castletown House 🏛	153 Cd21		www.irish-architecture.com/castletown
			http://kildare.ie
Cathair Saidhbhín ☐ 🏛	152 Ba25		www.cahersiveen.com
Céide Fields 🏛	150 Bc17		www.museumsofmayo.com/ceide.htm
			www.heritageireland.ie
Charles Fort 🏛	152 Bd26		www.kinsale.ie/kinshist.htm
			www.cork-guide.ie/charles.htm
			www.12travel.com/ie/attractions/charlesfort.html
Charleville Castle 🏛	153 Cb21		www.charlevillecastle.com
Cill Áirne ☐ 🏛	152 Bb25		www.killarney.ie
			www.killarneyonline.ie
			www.killarney-insight.com
Cill Chainnigh ☐ 🏛 🏛	153 Cb23		www.kilkenny.ie
			www.kilkennycoco.ie
			www.historic.irishcastles.com/kilkenny.htm
Cill Chaoi ☐ 🏛	152 Bb23		www.shannonregiontourism.ie
			www.12travel.ie/ie/Shannon/Kilkee.html
Cill Rois ☐ 🏛	152 Bb23		www.kilrush.ie
			www.kilrushcreekmarina.ie
Cionn tSáile ☐ 🏛 🏛	152 Bd26		www.kinsale.ie
			www.portkinsale.com
Clare	106		www.county-clare.com
Clare Abbey 🏛	152 Bc22		http://clare.goireland.com
Clare Island 🏛	150 Bb19		www.anu.ie/clareisland/welcome.htm
			www.mayo-ireland.ie/Mayo/Towns/clareisland/clareisland.htm
Classiebawn Castle 🏛	150 Ca17		www.sligozone.net/Mullaghmore.htm
Clear Island 🏛	152 Bb26		www.oilean-chleire.ie
Clew Bay 🏛	150 Bb19	52	www.museumsofmayo.com/clewbay.htm
Clifden Castle 🏛	150 Bb20	60	www.all-ireland.com/attractions/c/clifden-castle.htm
Cliffs of Moher 🏛	152 Bb22	104	www.burrenpage.com/CliffsofMoher.html
			www.ireland-west.com/cliffsofmoher.html
Cloich na Coillte ☐ 🏛	152 Bc26		www.clonakilty.ie
			www.clon.ie
			www.cork-guide.ie/clonakilty/clonakilty.htm
Clonakenny ☐ 🏛	153 Ca22		www.clonakilty.ie
			www.clon.ie
			www.cork-guide.ie/clonakilty/clonakilty.htm
Clonalis House 🏛	150 Bd19		www.clonalis.com
			www.hidden-ireland.com/clonalis.html
Clonca Cross 🏛	151 Cc15		www.megalithomania.com/show/site/1227
Clonfert Cathedral 🏛	152 Ca21		www.lawrencetown.com/clonfert.htm
Clonmacnoise 🏛	153 Ca21	92	www.moytura.com/clonmacnoise.htm
			www.heritageireland.ie
Clonmany ☐ 🏛	151 Cc15		www.clonmany.com
Clonmel ☐ 🏛	153 Ca24		www.clonmel.ie
			www.visitclonmel.com
			www.clonmel.info
Cluain Meala ☐ 🏛	152 Ca24		www.clonmel.ie
			www.visitclonmel.com
			www.clonmel.info
Cobh ☐ 🏛	152 Bd26		www.cobhheritage.com
Cong ☐ 🏛	150 Bc20		www.cong-ireland.com/home.htm
Conga ☐ 🏛	150 Bc20		www.cong-ireland.com/home.htm
Connacht	42		www.tourismireland.com/info
Connemara 🏛	150 Bb20	58	www.connemara-tourism.org
Connemara N. P. 🏛	150 Bb20	56	www.duchas.ie/en/NaturalHeritage
			http://homepage.tinet.ie/~knp/connemara/index.htm
Corcaigh ☐ 🏛 🏛	152 Bd26		www.corkcorp.ie
			www.cork-guide.ie
			www.corkracecourse.ie
Cork ☐ 🏛 🏛	152 Bd26	136	www.corkcorp.ie
			www.cork-guide.ie
Cormac's Chapel	112		www.tipp.ie/cashelsi.htm
			www.heritagetowns.com/cashel.html
County Museum 🏛	151 Cd19		www.dundalktown.ie/dundalktown/museo1.htm
Crag Cave 🏛	152 Bb24		www.cragcave.com
			www.showcaves.com/english/ie/showcaves/Crag.html
Craggaunowen Project 🏛	152 Bd22		www.shannonheritage.com/Craggaunowen_Day.htm
			www.stonepages.com/ireland/craggaunowen.html
Creevykeel 🏛	150 Ca17		www.stonepages.com/ireland/creevykeel.html
			http://irishmegaliths.megalithomania.com/zCreevykeel.htm
			http://indigo.ie/~jdem/Creevykeel%20home.html
Croagh Patrick 🏛	150 Bb19		www.croagh-patrick.com
Crookhaven ☐ 🏛	152 Ba26		www.crookhaven.ie/index.html
Croom Mills 🏛	152 Bd23		www.croommills.ie/index.asp
			www.shannonregiontourism.ie/detail.asp?memberID=13153
Culzean Castle 🏛	151 Dc15		www.culzeancastle.net
Curragh Chase Forest Park 🏛	152 Bc23		www.coillte.ie
Curragh Racetrack 🏛	153 Cc22		www.curragh.ie
Cushendall 🏛	151 Da15		www.northantrim.com/cushendall.htm
			www.antrim.net/cushendall
Cushendun ☐ 🏛 🏛	151 Da15		www.northantrim.com/cushendun.htm
			www.antrim.net/cushendun

Davagh Forest Park 🏛	151 Cd17		www.forestserviceni.gov.uk
Derry = Londonderry ☐ 🏛	151 Cc16		www.derryvisitor.com
Derrynane National Historic Park 🏛 🏛	152 Ba26	119	www.caherdanielonline.com
			www.12travel.co.uk/ie/attractions/derrynanehouse.html
Devenish Island 🏛	151 Cb17	36	www.enniskillen.com/devenish_island.htm
			www.emeraldtiger.com/countys/fermanagh/devenish.htm
Dinas Head 🏛	153 Db26		www.britainexpress.com/countryside/coast/dinas.htm
			www.westcountryviews.co.uk/coastal/dinas/dinas.htm
Dingle ☐ 🏛	152 Ba24	114	www.dingle-peninsula.ie/activities4.html
			www.emeraldtiger.com/countys/kerry/fungie.htm
Doe Castle 🏛		10	www.dun-na-ngall.com/doe.html
Donadea Forest Park 🏛	153 Cc21		www.coillte.ie/tourism_and_recreation/donadea.htm
Donegal ☐ 🏛	150 Ca16	10ff.	www.donegal.ie
			www.donegaltown.ie/Our_Towns.aspx
Donegal Castle 🏛	150 Ca16		www.ireland-now.com/castles/donegal.html
			www.heritageireland.ie
Doolin 🏛	152 Bc22	105	www.doolin-tourism.com
Down Cathedral 🏛	151 Da18		www.downcathedral.org
			www.visitdownpatrick.com/downcathedral.htm
Downpatrick ☐ 🏛	151 Da18		www.visitdownpatrick.com
Downpatrick Head 🏛	150 Bc17		www.castlebar.ie/clubs/mayo-birdwatch/galleries/downpatrick
			www.crossmolina.ie/images_pages/downpatrick.htm
			www.castlebar.ie/photos/the-west/downpatrick-head/glry
Drogheda ☐ 🏛 🏛	151 Cd20		www.drogheda-tourism.com
			www.solo.ie/samba
Droichead Átha ☐ 🏛 🏛	151 Cd20		www.drogheda-tourism.com
			www.solo.ie/samba
Drombeg Circle 🏛	152 Bc26		www.stonepages.com/ireland/drombeg.html
			http://easyweb.easynet.co.uk/~aburnham/ireland/drombeg.htm
Drum Manor Forest Park 🏛	151 Cd17		www.forestserviceni.gov.uk
Dublin ● 🏛 🏛	153 Cd21	70ff.	www.visitdublin.com
			www.dublincity.ie
			www.leopardstown.com
Dun Aengus Fort 🏛	152 Bb21		www.irish-society.org
			www.shee-eire.com
Dún An Rí Forest Park 🏛	151 Cc19		www.coillte.ie/tourism_and_recreation/dunanri.htm
Dún Fearbha/Dún Moher		66	www.12travel.de/ie/West/Inishmaan.html
Dun Laoghaire ☐ 🏛 🏛	153 Cd21	86	www.dun-laoghaire.com
			www.visitdublin.com/dunlaoghaire
Dun na nGall ☐ 🏛	150 Ca16		www.donegal.ie
			www.donegaltown.ie/Our_Towns.aspx
Dunbay Castle 🏛	152 Ba26		www.castletown.com/dunboycs.htm
			www.bearatourism.com/visitor/castle.html
Dunbeg Fort 🏛	152 Ad24		http://indigo.ie/~jdem/Dunbeg%20Kerry.htm
			http://home.comcast.net/~hories/Ireland/Dingle/Dingle.html
Dunbrody Abbey 🏛	153 Cc25		www.dunbrodyabbey.com
Dundrum Castle 🏛	151 Da18	40	www.ehsni.gov.uk/places/monuments/dundrum.shtml
			www.pdevlinz.btinternet.co.uk/dundrumcastle.htm
Dunguaire Castle 🏛	152 Bc21		www.kinvara.com/dunc.html
			www.gardensireland.com/dunguaire-castle.html
			www.shannonheritage.com/Dunguaire_Ban.htm
Dunluce Castle 🏛	151 Cd15	24	www.northantrim.com/dunlucecastle.htm
			www.emeraldtiger.com/countys/antrim/dunluce.htm
			www.heritageireland.ie
Dunmore Cave 🏛	153 Cb23		www.12travel.ie/South_East/attractions/dunmore_cave.html
Dunmore East ☐ 🏛	153 Cc25		www.waterford-dunmore.com
Dunsany Castle 🏛	151 Cd20		www.dunsany.net/castle1.htm
Emo Court 🏛	153 Cb22		www.heritageireland.ie/en/HistoricSites/East/EmoCourtLaois
			www.irelandseye.com
			www.laois.ie/heritagetrail/emo.html
Ennis ☐ 🏛	152 Bc22		www.ennis.ie/cgi-bin/eiat.cgi
Ennis Friary 🏛	152 Bc22		www.heritageireland.ie/en/HistoricSites/South/EnnisFriaryClare
			www.shannonregiontourism.ie/detail.asp?memberID=12196
Enniskerry ☐ 🏛	153 Cd22		www.enniskerry.ie
			www.irish-architecture.com
Enniskillen ☐ 🏛	151 Cb18		www.enniskillen.com
Enniskillen Castle 🏛	151 Cb18		www.enniskillencastle.co.uk
			www.enniskillen.com/enniskillen_castle.html
Eochaill ☐ 🏛 🏛	152 Ca26		www.youghal.ie
			www.cork-guide.ie/youghal.htm
Errew Abbey 🏛	150 Bc18		www.crossmolina.ie/errew.htm
			http://mayo.goireland.com
Fairyhouse Racetrack 🏛	153 Cd21		www.fairyhouseracecourse.ie
Fanad	151 Cb15	12	http://jlpourroy.com/fanad
Fanad Head	151 Cb15	12	www.ramelton.net/Trips/Fanad.htm
			www.lanternroom.com/lighthouses/ireland/ireld49.htm
Fanore ☐ 🏛	152 Bc21		www.fanorecottages.com/about.html
			www.wannasurf.com/spot/Europe/Ireland/West/fanore
Farran Forest Park 🏛	152 Bc26		www.coillte.ie/tourism_and_recreation/farran.htm
Fishguard ☐ 🏛	153 Db26		www.visitpembrokeshire.com/TIC/fishguard.asp
			www.visitpembrokeshire.com
Florence Court Forest Park 🏛	151 Cb18		www.forestserviceni.gov.uk
Florence Court House 🏛	150 Cb18		www.nationaltrust.org.uk
			www.enniskillen.com/florencecourthouse.html

From left to right: The Giant's Causeway; view of Glen Head; the Cathedral of Our Lady in Galway; Johnstown Castle; the Lakes of Killarney; the ruins on the Rock of Cashel.

From left to right: Waterford; Dunbrody Abbey; Staigue Fort, which is 2,000 years old; the monastic establishment on Skellig Michael; Westport House. Below: at Ballycrovane in Cork.

This edition is published on behalf of APA Publications GmbH & Co. Verlag KG, Singapore Branch, Singapore by Verlag Wolfgang Kunth GmbH & Co KG, Munich, Germany

Distributed in the United States by:

Langenscheidt Publishers, Inc.
36-36 33rd Street
Long Island City, NY 11106
Phone: 1-800-432-6277
www.Langenscheidt.com

ISBN 9-789812-58866-1

Original edition:
© 2007 Verlag Wolfgang Kunth GmbH & Co. KG, Munich
Königinstr. 11
80539 Munich
Ph: +49.89.45 80 20-0
Fax: +49.89.45 80 20-21
www.kunth-verlag.de

English edition:
Copyright © 2008 Verlag Wolfgang Kunth GmbH & Co. KG
© Cartography: GeoGraphic Publishers GmbH & Co. KG
Topographical Imaging MHM ® Copyright © Digital Wisdom, Inc.

Text: John Sykes, Köln
Translation: Dr. Joan Lawton Clough-Laub, JMS Books LLP

Printed in Slovakia

The information and facts presented in the book have been extensively researched and edited for accuracy. The publishers, authors, and editors, cannot, however, guarantee that all of the information in the book is entirely accurate or up to date at the time of publication. The publishers are grateful for any suggestions or corrections that would improve the content of this work.